patterns   grammar

graphs   **FLASH** charts

FLASH
FORWARD
TEST PREP

spelling   context

Written by **Kathy Furgang**

Illustrations by **Remy Simard**

P9-CCM-935

© 2008 by Flash Kids

All rights reserved. No part of this publication may be reproduced,
stored in a retrieval system, or transmitted, in any form or by any means,
electronic, mechanical, photocopying, recording, or otherwise,
without prior written permission from the publisher.

Cover illustration by Hector Borlasca
Cover design by Loira Walsh
Interior design by Gladys Lai
Edited by Eliza Berkowitz

Flash Kids
A Division of Barnes & Noble
122 Fifth Avenue
New York, NY 10011

ISBN: 978-1-4114-1618-5

Please submit all inquiries to FlashKids@bn.com

Printed and bound in the United States

1 3 5 7 9 10 8 6 4 2

Dear Parent,

Test taking can be challenging for kids. In the face of test questions, answer bubbles, and the ticking clock, it's easy to see why tests can be overwhelming. That's why it's vital that children prepare for tests beforehand. Knowing the material is only part of preparing for tests. It's equally important that children practice answering different types of questions, filling in answers, and pacing themselves through test material. Children who practice taking tests develop confidence and can relax during the real test.

This Flash Forward Test Prep book will give your child the opportunity to practice taking tests in reading and math. Each practice test is based on national standards, so you know your child is reviewing important material he or she should be learning in the fourth grade. In addition to reinforcing fourth-grade curriculum, this book allows your child to practice answering different kinds of test questions. Best of all, each unit ends with a four-page practice test that reviews all the material in that unit. This truly gives kids a chance to show what they know and to see their progress.

The more practice children have before taking a test, the more relaxed and confident they will be during the exam. As your child works through the book, he or she will start to develop test-taking strategies. These strategies can be utilized during a real test. By the time your child finishes the book, he or she will be ready to tackle any exam, from the annual standardized test to the weekly pop quiz!

Table of Contents

UNIT 2: Math

Section 4: Number Sense

Section 5: Algebra and Functions

Section 6: Measurement and Geometry

Section 7: Statistics, Data Analysis, and Probability

Section 8: Mathematical Reasoning

Section 9: Test

Test-Taking Tips

Preparing for a test starts with your mind and body. Here are some things you can do before the test to make sure you're ready.

- A few days before the test, get together with friends from your class to review the material. Have fun quizzing each other.

- The night before the test, go to bed early and get plenty of sleep.

- Eat a healthy breakfast the morning of the test.

- Find out beforehand if you need a pencil, eraser, or pen, and make sure you pack them in your schoolbag.

- Before you leave for school, do a few practice test questions at home to get warmed up.

- Remember to use the restroom before the test begins.

- Have confidence in yourself. A positive attitude will help you do well!

Once the test has started, you need to stay focused. Here are some tips to keep in mind during the test.

- Always begin by reading or listening carefully to the directions.

- Make sure you read all the answer choices before choosing the one you think is correct.

- If you get stuck on a certain question, it's okay to skip it. Go back to the question later.

- Work at your own pace. Don't pay attention to how quickly other students are completing the test.

- Fill in the answer bubbles completely and neatly.

- If you finish the test before time is up, use the time to review your answers.

- Take time to double check any questions you felt uncertain about. Make sure you want to stick with your answer.

Here are some tips to keep in mind when taking reading and language tests.

- Read each question or passage slowly and carefully.

- Say words in your head and think about the sounds.

- Underline important words in the question that tell you what you need to do.

- As you read a passage, underline key words and phrases.

- Use context clues to help figure out the meaning of a word you might not know.

- Cross out answers you know are wrong. Then focus on the remaining choices.

- It's okay to go back to the passage or sentence and reread it.

These tips will help you as you work on math tests.

- Find out if you can use a piece of scratch paper or part of the test booklet to work through math problems.

- Make sure you understand each question before you choose an answer. Reread the question if you need to.

- Solve a problem twice and make sure you get the same answer both times.

- Try plugging in the answer choices to see which one makes a true math sentence.

- When you're solving word problems or story problems, underline key words that tell you what to do.

- Draw a picture to help you visualize the right answer.

- Pay attention to the operation signs and make sure you know if you need to add, subtract, multiply, or divide.

Section 1: Reading
Main Idea
Read the passage and answer the questions.

The Grand Canyon

Each year the Grand Canyon gets about 5 million visitors, and it's easy to understand why. The Grand Canyon really is grand. It takes up over a million acres in northwestern Arizona and is about 5,000 feet deep. The deepest part of the canyon is 6,000 feet deep. The widest part is 18 miles from side to side.

Scientists have found out a lot about the Grand Canyon. The oldest rocks in the canyon are close to 2 billion years old. The canyon formed by erosion. If you look at the canyon from above, you can see how the Colorado River has made a deep carve into the earth.

The Grand Canyon is home to thousands of plants and animals. Many people have lived in the canyon as well. The oldest human artifacts are almost 12,000 years old. They include handmade animal figures, baskets, and simple tools.

1. What is the main idea of the passage?
  Ⓐ The Grand Canyon is 5,000 feet deep.
  Ⓑ The Grand Canyon is an interesting place.
  Ⓒ The Colorado River runs through the canyon.
  Ⓓ The oldest human artifact in the canyon is 12,000 years old.

2. Where can you find the main idea written?
  Ⓐ in the first sentence
  Ⓑ in the last sentence
  Ⓒ in the second paragraph
  Ⓓ The main idea is not stated in exact words.

3. Which sentence does **not** help support the main idea?
  Ⓐ The canyon formed by erosion.
  Ⓑ Each year the Grand Canyon gets about 5 million visitors, and it's easy to understand why.
  Ⓒ The deepest part of the canyon is 6,000 feet deep.
  Ⓓ The oldest human artifacts are almost 12,000 years old.

4. Which sentence is the main idea of paragraph 2?
  Ⓐ sentence 1
  Ⓑ sentence 2
  Ⓒ sentence 3
  Ⓓ sentence 4

Evaluating Characters

Read the story and answer the questions.

Get Set, Go!

It was Track and Field Day at Marlboro Elementary School. Becky and Mike stood at the starting line waiting for the race to begin. Becky had been waiting for this race for what seemed like an eternity. She was the fastest runner in her class and she knew the only challenge would be beating Mike.

Mike was the fastest runner in *his* class, and he knew that Becky was his greatest competitor. They looked at each other as the other runners gathered around them, stretching to warm their muscles.

"Good luck," Mike said to Becky.

"Right," Becky answered. "Good luck to you too." Becky looked down at her toes. Soon the race would be over and the whole school would know who the fastest runner was.

Mike wiggled his feet to keep them warmed up.

"Attention!" said the announcer through the loudspeaker. The butterflies in Mike's stomach fluttered and Becky's heart raced. The crowd cheered that the race was ready to begin. "On your mark," he announced. "Get set, Go!"

1. Who is the main character in the story?
  Ⓐ Becky
  Ⓑ Mike
  Ⓒ Becky and Mike
  Ⓓ the announcer

2. Which word **best** describes how Becky is feeling?
  Ⓐ angry
  Ⓑ happy
  Ⓒ sad
  Ⓓ nervous

3. Which word **best** describes how Mike is feeling?
  Ⓐ angry
  Ⓑ happy
  Ⓒ sad
  Ⓓ nervous

4. Why do you think the characters wish each other luck before the race starts?
  Ⓐ They want to confuse each other.
  Ⓑ They want to show good sportsmanship.
  Ⓒ They want the other person to win.
  Ⓓ They were told to say it by their coach.

Evaluating Information

Read the passage and answer the questions.

Sally Ride

In 1983, Sally Ride became the first American woman to travel to outer space. At the age of 32, she was also the youngest person to reach outer space. Ride joined the NASA program in 1978. She responded to a newspaper advertisement looking for people to join the space program. She was part of the first class of NASA astronauts to accept women.

As part of her training, she worked on developing a robot arm for the space shuttle. When she rode the space shuttle *Challenger* in 1983, she was the first to use that robot arm. The arm was used to retrieve a satellite from space. The next year she traveled aboard the *Challenger* again. In all, Ride spent more than 343 hours in space.

Today, Sally Ride has her own company that focuses on bringing interesting science programs to young people. She is especially interested in getting young girls to become interested in science.

1. When did Sally Ride decide to become an astronaut?
Ⓐ 1983
Ⓑ 1978
Ⓒ 1943
Ⓓ 1932

2. Which fact about Sally Ride is **not** true?
Ⓐ She was the first American woman to travel to space.
Ⓑ She was the youngest person to travel to space.
Ⓒ She was the first astronaut to go to the moon.
Ⓓ She rode in the space shuttle *Challenger*.

3. What did Sally Ride do as part of her training?
Ⓐ She answered a newspaper advertisement.
Ⓑ She retrieved a satellite from space.
Ⓒ She developed a robot arm.
Ⓓ She taught young people about science.

4. How did Sally Ride find out that NASA was beginning to allow women to become astronauts?
Ⓐ She was contacted by NASA.
Ⓑ She read a newspaper advertisement.
Ⓒ She called NASA on the phone.
Ⓓ Her mother told her about it.

Comparing and Contrasting

Read the story and answer the questions.

The Leaf Pile

Luis raked up the last few leaves of the season. He had worked all morning so that he could spend the afternoon at the park with his friends.

"Cannonball!" came a scream from behind him. His little brother, Tony, ran and jumped into his giant pile of leaves, sending them flying in all directions. As he bounced in the pile, he let out a joyful giggle.

Luis was angry. It had taken him all morning to rake that pile. "Get out of there," he yelled at Tony. "You ruined my pile of leaves!"

"Come play in the leaves with me," said Tony. He reached up, grabbed Luis by the arm, and pulled him into the pile. Luis could not help but laugh when he landed in the pile with a crunch.

"Yeah!" said Tony. "Isn't it fun?"

Luis never went to the park that day. Instead, he spent all afternoon playing in the leaves with Tony.

1. Luis is responsible. How can Tony be described differently from his brother?
Ⓐ Tony is angry.
Ⓑ Tony is carefree.
Ⓒ Tony is bored.
Ⓓ Tony is talented.

2. In what way are Luis and Tony the same?
Ⓐ They are the same age.
Ⓑ They are the same person.
Ⓒ They have the same chores to do.
Ⓓ They are part of the same family.

3. What does Tony do that Luis did **not** want to do?
Ⓐ play in the leaves
Ⓑ go to the park
Ⓒ rake the leaves
Ⓓ play with his friends

4. Which brother would be **more likely** to want to play in the snow all day?
Ⓐ Luis
Ⓑ Tony
Ⓒ both Luis and Tony
Ⓓ neither Luis and Tony

Context Clues

Read the passage and answer the questions.

Maple Syrup

What do you pour on your pancakes? Where does this sweet liquid come from? It is called maple syrup, and it is taken directly from a maple tree.

To collect the syrup, a tap, or pipe, is put through the bark of a maple tree until it reaches the wood inside. Sap then runs through the tap. Canada is the biggest producer of maple syrup. In the United States, most syrup is produced in Vermont, Maine, New York, and Ohio.

Most maple syrup is collected in the late winter and early spring. That's because the sap flows when it is freezing at night and warmer during the days.

The sap is then boiled until the water evaporates and just the syrup is left. It takes about 40 liters of sap to make just one liter of maple syrup!

1. According to the passage, what is the meaning of *tap?*
   Ⓐ dance
   Ⓑ pipe
   Ⓒ water
   Ⓓ instrument

2. According to the passage, what is *sap?*
   Ⓐ a liquid
   Ⓑ a solid
   Ⓒ a gas
   Ⓓ none of the above

3. What does *producer* mean?
   Ⓐ a kind of syrup
   Ⓑ a state or country
   Ⓒ a maker
   Ⓓ a kind of pancake

4. What does *flows* mean?
   Ⓐ rolls
   Ⓑ moves like a liquid
   Ⓒ follows
   Ⓓ stops moving

5. What does *evaporates* mean?
   Ⓐ removing of a liquid
   Ⓑ removing of a solid
   Ⓒ removing of a gas
   Ⓓ none of the above

Inferring Supporting Details

Read the story and answer the questions.

Puzzle Trouble

I got many presents on my birthday. My favorite was the Manny Martian puzzle. I love the Manny Martian show! I had hoped to get the puzzle from Mom and Dad and put it together on the night of my birthday. Then I would glue the pieces down onto a board and display it in my room.

Of course, things did not go as planned. Sure, I got the puzzle, but there were three pieces missing. I had to wait six weeks to get a new one from the Manny Martian company. Then the pieces wouldn't stick to the glue and the board. They kept falling into the fish tank when I put the puzzle on the wall. My birthday was three months ago and I'm still having puzzle trouble!

The Manny Martian show is on tonight. I don't think I feel like watching.

1. How did the narrator hope to get the puzzle he wanted?
   Ⓐ He wanted to get it from his parents for his birthday.
   Ⓑ He wanted to buy it in a store.
   Ⓒ He wanted to order it from the company that makes it.
   Ⓓ He wanted to get it from a friend at his party.

2. What happened that did **not** go as planned for the narrator?
   Ⓐ He did not get the puzzle.
   Ⓑ There were pieces missing from the puzzle.
   Ⓒ The puzzle was too hard for him to put together.
   Ⓓ There was no room on his wall to put the puzzle.

3. What did the narrator get in the mail from the Manny Martian company?
   Ⓐ glue and a wooden board
   Ⓑ a fish tank
   Ⓒ a new puzzle
   Ⓓ a birthday cake

4. What did the narrator's experience make him think about the Manny Martian show?
   Ⓐ He liked the show even more after getting the puzzle.
   Ⓑ He did not feel like watching the show after having the puzzle problem.
   Ⓒ He showed the program to all of his friends.
   Ⓓ His opinion of the show did not change.

Audience and Purpose

Read the passage and answer the questions.

Lance Armstrong

When people think of professional bike racing, one name comes to mind: Lance Armstrong. That name also comes to mind when people think of beating the odds and fighting cancer.

Armstrong was already a championship cyclist when he was diagnosed with cancer in 1996. After successfully treating the cancer, he got back on his bike. In 1999, he won the most famous race in biking, the Tour de France. He won the race seven years in a row, from 1999 to 2005.

Lance Armstrong has been a great example for people who have challenges to overcome. He has shown that with hard work, a person can succeed.

Since 2004, the Lance Armstrong Foundation has sold yellow rubber wristbands that say "Livestrong." The wristbands have raised more than 63 million dollars for cancer research and programs. They represent the fight against cancer and the search to find a cure.

1. What is the main purpose of the passage?
- Ⓐ to inform people about Lance Armstrong
- Ⓑ to entertain people with facts about biking
- Ⓒ to entertain people with facts about fighting cancer
- Ⓓ to persuade people to take up bicycling for exercise

2. Who do you think would be the **best** audience for this passage?
- Ⓐ a person who wants to learn how to bike
- Ⓑ a doctor who is looking for cures for cancer
- Ⓒ a person who is inspired by the dedication of others
- Ⓓ a person who wants to attend the Tour de France

3. What might be another purpose of this passage?
- Ⓐ to inform people about cancer awareness
- Ⓑ to persuade people to support the Lance Armstrong Foundation
- Ⓒ to inform people about the importance of working hard
- Ⓓ all of the above

4. How does the Lance Armstrong Foundation help the fight against cancer?
- Ⓐ It participates in the Tour de France.
- Ⓑ It supports Lance Armstrong's sports career.
- Ⓒ It sells "Livestrong" bracelets to earn money for cancer research.
- Ⓓ It sells "Livestrong" bracelets to support the Tour de France.

Understanding Genre Features

Read the story and answer the questions.

How Cindy Became a Duck Princess

Once upon a time there was a duck named Cindy. Cindy was a beautiful duck. She lived with her wicked stepmother duck and her three wicked stepsister ducks. Cindy caught food for the wicked ducks. She cleaned their nests for them. The other ducks just swam around in the pond and looked at their reflections in the water all day. They were all quite ugly compared to Cindy, who had beautiful brown and black feathers.

One day the ducks got an invitation to a grand ball on the pond. At the ball, Cindy won the heart of a handsome duck prince. The ugly ducks were jealous. Cindy and the prince got married, and now Cindy is the princess of the pond. Now all the other ducks must clean her nest while she stares at *her* reflection in the pond all day.

1. What is the genre of this story?
Ⓐ fairy tale
Ⓑ poem
Ⓒ nonfiction
Ⓓ biography

2. Who is the main character of the story?
Ⓐ Cindy
Ⓑ Cindy's stepmother
Ⓒ Cindy's stepsisters
Ⓓ the handsome duck prince

3. What is the **best** description of the characters in the story?
Ⓐ They are all good.
Ⓑ They are all evil.
Ⓒ They are all ducks.
Ⓓ They are all swans.

4. What are the forces of good and evil in the story?
Ⓐ Cindy is evil; her stepsisters and stepmother are evil.
Ⓑ Cindy is good; her stepsisters and stepmother are evil.
Ⓒ Cindy is good; the duck prince is evil.
Ⓓ Cindy is evil; the duck prince is good.

5. What happens to Cindy at the end of the story?
Ⓐ She goes to a ball.
Ⓑ She cleans the nests of her stepsisters.
Ⓒ She becomes a duck princess.
Ⓓ She becomes a human princess.

6. What fairy tale does this story sound most like?
Ⓐ Beauty and the Beast
Ⓑ Snow White and the Seven Dwarfs
Ⓒ Goldilocks and the Three Bears
Ⓓ Cinderella

Sequencing

Read the passage and answer the questions.

How to Do Your Own Laundry

Your parents may have washed your clothes since you were a baby. Do you know how to do your own laundry?

First, you take the pile of clothes you need to wash and separate them by color. Separating the dark fabrics from the light ones will keep the colors looking good.

Then, put a load of clothes into the machine and add detergent to the detergent compartment. Read the bottle to tell you how much soap to add. Choose a medium or cool temperature to help keep clothes from shrinking in the heat. Start the machine and come back 30 to 40 minutes later. If the machine has finished, move the clothes into the dryer and set it according to the directions. After the dryer is finished, remove and fold the clothes as quickly as you can. This will keep the clothes from wrinkling.

1. What is the first thing to do if you wash your own clothes?
- Ⓐ Separate the clothes by color.
- Ⓑ Gather the clothes that need to be washed.
- Ⓒ Add soap to the machine.
- Ⓓ Read the directions on the dryer.

2. What is the next thing to do when washing your own clothes?
- Ⓐ Separate the clothes by color.
- Ⓑ Gather the clothes that need to be washed.
- Ⓒ Add soap to the machine.
- Ⓓ Read the directions on the dryer.

3. Why should a medium or cool temperature be set on the washing machine?
- Ⓐ to keep the colors looking good
- Ⓑ to keep the clothes from wrinkling
- Ⓒ to keep the clothes from shrinking
- Ⓓ A medium or cool temperature is not recommended.

4. What should happen after the dryer is finished running?
- Ⓐ The clothes should be moved to the dryer.
- Ⓑ The clothes should be folded.
- Ⓒ The clothes should be washed again.
- Ⓓ The clothes should be separated.

Evaluating Supporting Details

Read the story and answer the questions.

The New Kid on the Bus

Today Mike saw a new face when he got on the bus. Mike introduced himself and learned that the new boy's name was Allen. Allen's family had just moved to the neighborhood from the next town over. Allen had to switch schools. He was not happy to leave his old class of friends, but he was eager to make new ones.

After chatting on the bus, Mike and Allen realized they had a lot in common. They lived only two blocks away from each other. They each had a younger brother who just happened to be named Mark. Also, they both loved baseball. Allen was on the local Little League team, just like Mike. Now that Allen's family had moved, Allen would be on Mike's team. Mike was glad he decided to sit down next to Allen that morning on the bus.

1. Why had Mike never seen Allen on the bus before?
   - Ⓐ Mike had never paid attention to the other kids before.
   - Ⓑ Mike was forced to move to a new seat because he misbehaved.
   - Ⓒ Allen was forced to move to a new seat because he misbehaved.
   - Ⓓ Allen was a new student at the school.

2. How did Allen feel about having to leave his old class?
   - Ⓐ glad
   - Ⓑ upset
   - Ⓒ He had mixed feelings.
   - Ⓓ We cannot know from reading the story.

3. Which thing below did Mike and Allen **not** have in common?
   - Ⓐ They lived two blocks from each other.
   - Ⓑ They both spoke Spanish.
   - Ⓒ They both had a younger brother named Mark.
   - Ⓓ They both loved baseball.

4. What else would happen as a result of Allen's family moving?
   - Ⓐ Allen and Mike would be in the same classes at school.
   - Ⓑ Allen and Mike would be on the same Little League team.
   - Ⓒ Allen and Mike would be in the same lunch period.
   - Ⓓ Allen and Mike would be in the same gym class.

Persuasive Writing

Read the letter and answer the questions.

The Hamster Request

Dear Mom and Dad,

I am writing this letter in hopes of convincing you to get me a pet hamster. With my birthday coming soon, I feel now is an appropriate time to give you my reasons why I think you should get me a hamster as a present.

I am allergic to dogs, and even though I love them they are out of the question. I did consider a cat for a while, but decided that it may be too hard to care for. I researched hamsters and found that they are very easy to care for. They need simple tap water and just a little food. We will have to purchase a small cage and some wood chips for the bottom of it. I will gladly handle all the daily chores with the hamster and clean its cage.

I hope you will give me an extra happy birthday this year. I want a hamster so badly. The name I picked for it is Nibbles.

Love,
Tammy

1. Who is making the request in the letter?
Ⓐ Tammy
Ⓑ Mom
Ⓒ Dad
Ⓓ the hamster

2. What method did the writer choose for making the request?
Ⓐ writing a birthday list
Ⓑ writing a letter
Ⓒ making a phone call
Ⓓ asking in person

3. Why doesn't the writer of the letter want a dog or cat?
Ⓐ She is allergic to dogs.
Ⓑ Cats are too difficult.
Ⓒ both A and B
Ⓓ The passage does not give this information.

4. Which is something a hamster will **not** need?
Ⓐ food and water
Ⓑ a leash
Ⓒ a cage
Ⓓ wood chips

Fact and Opinion

Read the passage and answer the questions.

The Eagle vs. The Turkey

The father of our country, Benjamin Franklin, would have liked the wild turkey to be our national symbol instead of the bald eagle. In a letter to his daughter in 1784, Franklin compared the eagle to the turkey. He said the eagle was "a bird of bad moral character. He does not get his living honestly." He explained that eagles steal food from other birds because they are too lazy to catch their own meals.

He goes on to say, "For the truth the turkey is in comparison a much more respectable bird." He described the way a wild turkey will attack to protect his home, much like an American who must protect himself from the British.

Although Ben Franklin had many great ideas, most people will agree that the bald eagle is the better choice as the national symbol.

1. What was Ben Franklin's opinion in the passage?
   Ⓐ The bald eagle is a good national symbol.
   Ⓑ The wild turkey should have been chosen as the national symbol.
   Ⓒ The bald eagle is a brave bird.
   Ⓓ The turkey is a weak bird.

2. Which statement from the passage is a fact?
   Ⓐ The eagle is a bird of bad moral character.
   Ⓑ The eagle does not make its living honestly.
   Ⓒ The turkey is a respectable bird.
   Ⓓ Franklin wrote to his daughter in 1784.

3. Which is a fact from the passage?
   Ⓐ Franklin compared the characteristics of an eagle and a turkey.
   Ⓑ Turkeys attack.
   Ⓒ Eagles steal.
   Ⓓ Eagles are lazy.

4. Which statement is an opinion of the author of the passage?
   Ⓐ Franklin made good points in his letter.
   Ⓑ The country needs a strong symbol.
   Ⓒ Ben Franklin had many great ideas.
   Ⓓ Other birds do not like eagles.

5. What does the author think the reader's opinion will be?
   Ⓐ The turkey is the better choice as the American symbol.
   Ⓑ The eagle is the better choice as the American symbol.
   Ⓒ Both choices are equally good.
   Ⓓ Neither is a good choice.

6. Which statement is a fact?
   Ⓐ The turkey is a symbol of America.
   Ⓑ The eagle is a symbol of America.
   Ⓒ Everyone likes the eagle as the symbol of America.
   Ⓓ Everyone would like to change the symbol of America.

Figurative Language

Read the story and answer the questions.

At the Beach

We were as happy as clams to go to the beach today. We packed up our bags and our swimsuits and marched out to the bus. Mom led our parade like a happy soldier.

When we got to the beach though, we got more than we bargained for. The sun was hot enough to melt a rock. Dad acted as though we were snowmen in the desert.

We all jumped into the water for some relief. It was just what the doctor ordered. I stayed in that cool water all day. I came out just to have some lunch. Mom had packed some of the comforts of home. We had peanut butter and jelly sandwiches and cookies. Then I went right back into the water.

When it was finally time to go home, my fingers looked like shriveled raisins from being in the water for so long.

1. What does the phrase *as happy as clams* mean?

  Ⓐ not happy at all

  Ⓑ a little bit happy

  Ⓒ very happy

  Ⓓ cannot tell

2. How did mom lead the family to the bus?

  Ⓐ in a happy, yet organized way

  Ⓑ in a happy, yet disorganized way

  Ⓒ in a strict way that was no fun for the family

  Ⓓ in a cautious way

3. How did the family get *more than they bargained for?*

  Ⓐ They placed bets about their day at the beach.

  Ⓑ The beach was not what they expected.

  Ⓒ The beach was exactly what they expected.

  Ⓓ They never found the beach.

4. What would it be like to be *a snowman in the desert?*

  Ⓐ It is not possible to tell.

  Ⓑ The snowman would be too hot in the desert.

  Ⓒ The snowman would be too cold in the desert.

  Ⓓ A desert would be a great place for a snowman.

Responding to Literature

Read the story and answer the questions.

Snow Day

Jenna woke up on Monday morning to the sound of her ringing alarm clock. She shot up out of bed. Had it snowed? Would there be school? She ran to the window. Before she even reached the windowsill, she could see the blinding white light peering through the curtain. *Yes*, she thought to herself. *Snow day!*

Just then, the phone rang and Jenna could hear her mother talking to the person on the other end of the line. "OK," her mom said. "Thanks for calling." She hung up and yelled "Snow day!" up the stairs to Jenna, who ran down to hug her mom.

"I knew it!" she cheered. Her dad was putting on his boots to shovel the driveway and her mom was heading into the kitchen to make hot chocolate for everyone. Jenna stared out the sliding glass door that led to the backyard. *Today is the day that the world's biggest snowman will be born*, she decided.

1. What word **best** describes the way Jenna felt about having a snow day?

Ⓐ angry
Ⓑ pleased
Ⓒ thrilled
Ⓓ confused

2. How did the family find out that there would be no school?

Ⓐ Someone called on the phone.
Ⓑ Someone came to the door.
Ⓒ Mom looked up the information on the computer.
Ⓓ Mom heard the news on television.

3. What made Jenna think there would be a snow day?

Ⓐ She was cold under the covers of her bed.
Ⓑ She saw the snow out her window.
Ⓒ She had a dream that it would snow.
Ⓓ She did not think there would be a snow day.

4. Why was Jenna's dad putting on his boots?

Ⓐ He was going skiing.
Ⓑ He was going to make a snowman.
Ⓒ He was going to shovel the snow.
Ⓓ He was not putting his boots on.

Evaluating Nonfiction

Read the passage and answer the questions.

Mount Rushmore

In 1924, historian Doane Robinson had an idea to build a monument in the Black Hills of South Dakota. The project was designed to attract more tourists to this area. A large piece of granite was chosen to be the site for the project.

It was decided that the faces of George Washington, Thomas Jefferson, Theodore Roosevelt, and Abraham Lincoln would be carved into the rock. The faces represent the first 150 years of American history.

Work on the monument began in 1927 and was completed in 1941. The monument covers more than 1,200 acres. Almost 3 million people visit Mount Rushmore each year. Some visitors are even lucky enough to see it being cleaned. Workers hang from ropes and scrub the presidents' faces with brushes and brooms!

1. What kind of rock is Mount Rushmore made of?
   Ⓐ black hills
   Ⓑ granite
   Ⓒ marble
   Ⓓ sandstone

2. Which of these presidents was **not** carved in Mount Rushmore?
   Ⓐ George Washington
   Ⓑ Thomas Jefferson
   Ⓒ Franklin D. Roosevelt
   Ⓓ Abraham Lincoln

3. Why was the monument built?
   Ⓐ to honor American presidents
   Ⓑ to attract tourists
   Ⓒ both A and B
   Ⓓ neither A or B

4. What can some tourists see while they visit the monument?
   Ⓐ They can see other sculptures of presidents.
   Ⓑ They can see workers cleaning the monument.
   Ⓒ They can see sculptors making new monuments.
   Ⓓ They can see people climb the statues.

5. About how many people visit the monument each year?
   Ⓐ 2 million
   Ⓑ 3 million
   Ⓒ 4 million
   Ⓓ 5 million

Comparing Across Texts

Read the passage and answer the questions.

Crazy Horse Memorial

Just 17 miles away from the Mount Rushmore memorial in South Dakota's Black Hills, sits the Crazy Horse Memorial. The project was started in 1948 and is still far from being finished. The monument honors the Lakota warrior, Crazy Horse.

When Mount Rushmore was being built, many Lakota in the area were upset. An American monument was being built on grounds that were sacred to many Native Americans. Some Lakota do not want the Crazy Horse Memorial to be finished. They think that this type of memorial will change the natural features of the land, just as Mount Rushmore did.

If the sculpture is finished, it will be the largest in the world. More than a million people already visit the site each year.

1. How does this passage relate to the passage "Mount Rushmore" on page 22?
   Ⓐ They are both about famous sculptors.
   Ⓑ They are both about American presidents.
   Ⓒ They are both about monuments built in the Black Hills of South Dakota.
   Ⓓ The passages are not related.

2. Where does this passage refer to Mount Rushmore?
   Ⓐ in the first paragraph
   Ⓑ in the second paragraph
   Ⓒ in both the first and the second paragraphs
   Ⓓ It does not mention Mount Rushmore.

3. Which passage discusses a monument that honors important people?
   Ⓐ "Mount Rushmore"
   Ⓑ "Crazy Horse Memorial"
   Ⓒ neither
   Ⓓ both

4. Which passage discusses the ideas of the Lakota Native American tribes?
   Ⓐ "Mount Rushmore"
   Ⓑ "Crazy Horse Memorial"
   Ⓒ neither
   Ⓓ both

5. Which passage discusses the sculptors who made the statues?
   Ⓐ "Mount Rushmore"
   Ⓑ "Crazy Horse Memorial"
   Ⓒ neither
   Ⓓ both

Setting

Read the story and answer the questions.

Life on Alpha 10

Life is good here. We float around the cabin all morning. Mom makes us pancakes by pushing the "serve pancakes" button on her Extreme Cooker 3000. Life in space has been great since we got here last week.

I have to start space school tomorrow. The school bus will pick me up by landing on the roof of our space house. Then I will shoot up to the roof in the Gravity Eraser and land right in seat 23 of the bus.

Mom says we can stay here as long as we want. Dad's new job at the space station is going well. I don't think we'll ever have to go back to earth. I will be happy as long as my old friends from school can be seen on the Telephone Monitor. Maybe someday my new friends and my old friends can see each other on the monitor.

1. What is the time setting of the story?
  Ⓐ past
  Ⓑ present
  Ⓒ future
  Ⓓ cannot tell

2. Where does the story take place?
  Ⓐ on a farm
  Ⓑ in space
  Ⓒ in the ocean
  Ⓓ under the ground

3. How can the reader tell that the story takes place in another time?
  Ⓐ We do not have Extreme Cooker 3000s.
  Ⓑ We do not have Gravity Erasers.
  Ⓒ We do not have telephone monitors.
  Ⓓ all of the above

4. Why do you think the family in the story is in space?
  Ⓐ The narrator's dad has to work on a space station.
  Ⓑ The narrator's mom wanted a change.
  Ⓒ The schools in space are better than on earth.
  Ⓓ The family likes an adventure.

5. How would the passage be different if it took place in another time?
  Ⓐ It would be exactly the same story.
  Ⓑ Most of the details of the story would be the same.
  Ⓒ The details of the story would be different.
  Ⓓ It is not possible to say.

Main Idea and Supporting Details

Read the passage and answer the questions.

Polar Bears

What animal weighs 400 to 1,300 pounds and lives in the Arctic? It is the polar bear! This bear is well adapted to such a cold climate. The animal's white fur helps it blend into its snowy environment. Underneath that fur the animal has black skin, not white. The dark skin helps absorb sunlight in this cold climate. The polar bear also has layers of blubber under its skin to keep it warm. The polar bear's thick fur is like wearing a heavy winter coat.

The polar bear spends time on land as well as in the sea and on ice. The habitat of the polar bear is becoming threatened. A gradual increase in temperature has caused the Arctic region to change. Ice caps are melting, and the polar bear's home is shrinking. Scientists predict the number of polar bears will decrease by two-thirds by the middle of this century.

1. What is the main idea of the first paragraph?
Ⓐ The polar bear spends time on land and at sea.
Ⓑ The polar bear has layers of blubber.
Ⓒ The polar bear's habitat is changing.
Ⓓ The polar bear is well adapted for the cold.

2. What is the main idea of the second paragraph?
Ⓐ The polar bear spends time on land and at sea.
Ⓑ The polar bear has layers of blubber.
Ⓒ The polar bear's habitat is changing.
Ⓓ The polar bear is well adapted for the cold.

3. Which detail in the passage refers to the polar bear's size?
Ⓐ Its white fur blends into its snowy environment.
Ⓑ It has black skin under its white fur.
Ⓒ It weighs 400 to 1,300 pounds.
Ⓓ It has layers of blubber to keep it warm.

4. Which detail describes how the polar bear's climate is changing?
Ⓐ The number of polar bears may decrease two-thirds by the middle of the century.
Ⓑ The polar bear's habitat is being threatened.
Ⓒ Polar bears spend time on land as well as in the sea and on ice.
Ⓓ Ice caps are melting, and the polar bear's home is shrinking.

Inferences

Read the story and answer the questions.

It's Almost Time!

"Get dressed," called Monica. "People will be here any minute." Josh wondered where the time went. It seemed like just a minute ago he was making ice in the ice cube trays and putting plastic cups on the table.

"Close the curtains too," Monica added. "We don't want the decorations to be seen from the street." Josh peeked out the window for cars and then quickly shut the curtains. *This was going to be a fun afternoon*, he thought.

"I'll put the cake on the big table and I'll look for the candles," said Josh.

"Not until you get dressed!" repeated Monica. "You look like you just rolled out of bed." Josh looked down at himself. He was still wearing his pajamas! He forgot that he started cleaning the house as soon as he woke up this morning. He did not want their guests to see him in pajamas!

1. What are Monica and Josh getting ready for?
   Ⓐ a test
   Ⓑ a party
   Ⓒ breakfast
   Ⓓ dinner

2. Why doesn't Monica want the decorations to be seen from the street?
   Ⓐ Decorations are not allowed in their house.
   Ⓑ She does not want people to come to their house.
   Ⓒ They are probably planning a surprise for someone.
   Ⓓ Monica is trying to be mean to Josh.

3. Why do you think Monica and Josh will need a cake and candles?
   Ⓐ They are hungry.
   Ⓑ It is someone's birthday.
   Ⓒ It is Labor Day.
   Ⓓ It is time for dessert.

4. Why did Josh **not** change his clothes in the morning?
   Ⓐ He forgot because he was busy cleaning.
   Ⓑ He planned to have guests see him in his pajamas.
   Ⓒ He forgot because he overslept.
   Ⓓ He thought he would be more comfortable in his pajamas.

Section 2: Written and Oral Language Conventions

Word Usage

Answer the questions below.

1. Which sentence uses the word *distribute* correctly?
Ⓐ I will distribute the cake to the oven.
Ⓑ I will distribute the tests to the students.
Ⓒ I will distribute the garbage to the garbage can.
Ⓓ I will distribute the bed to the sleep.

2. Which sentence uses the word *contaminated* correctly?
Ⓐ The paper was contaminated with ink.
Ⓑ The paper was contaminated with time.
Ⓒ The paper was contaminated with air.
Ⓓ The paper was contaminated with germs.

3. Which sentence uses the word *elaborate* correctly?
Ⓐ The jewelry was elaborate.
Ⓑ The dirt was elaborate.
Ⓒ The water was elaborate.
Ⓓ The puppy was elaborate.

4. Which sentence uses the word *gag* correctly?
Ⓐ He played a gag on me.
Ⓑ I thought I would gag on the food.
Ⓒ both
Ⓓ neither

5. Which sentence uses the word *indicated* correctly?
Ⓐ He indicated sleep.
Ⓑ She indicated time.
Ⓒ They indicated that they were lost.
Ⓓ She indicated extra time.

6. Which sentence uses the word *vacant* correctly?
Ⓐ The parking lot was vacant.
Ⓑ The bottle was vacant.
Ⓒ The stone was vacant.
Ⓓ The nail was vacant.

7. Which sentence uses the word *complicated* correctly?
Ⓐ The paper clip is complicated.
Ⓑ The homework is complicated.
Ⓒ The backpack is complicated.
Ⓓ The pencil is complicated.

8. Which sentence uses the word *dispatched* correctly?
Ⓐ The book was dispatched from my hands.
Ⓑ The toy was dispatched from the box.
Ⓒ The boy was dispatched from the bath.
Ⓓ The bus was dispatched from the station.

Synonyms and Antonyms

Answer the questions below.

1. Which word means the same as *discover?*
  Ⓐ tie
  Ⓑ loose
  Ⓒ find
  Ⓓ treat

2. Which word has a meaning most similar to *tempt?*
  Ⓐ attract
  Ⓑ create
  Ⓒ forget
  Ⓓ uncover

3. Which word means the opposite of *dangerously?*
  Ⓐ small
  Ⓑ grand
  Ⓒ danger
  Ⓓ safely

4. Which word is an antonym for *opinion?*
  Ⓐ thought
  Ⓑ fact
  Ⓒ idea
  Ⓓ talk

5. Which word is a synonym for *dialogue?*
  Ⓐ speech
  Ⓑ punctuation
  Ⓒ terror
  Ⓓ mask

6. Which word means the opposite of *freezing?*
  Ⓐ warm
  Ⓑ cold
  Ⓒ burning
  Ⓓ cooking

7. Which word is an antonym for *responsible?*
  Ⓐ irreverent
  Ⓑ irresponsible
  Ⓒ trustworthy
  Ⓓ trusting

8. Which word has the same meaning as *crate?*
  Ⓐ grate
  Ⓑ satchel
  Ⓒ box
  Ⓓ screen

9. Which word is an antonym for *tardy?*
  Ⓐ early
  Ⓑ late
  Ⓒ ready
  Ⓓ present

10. Which word is a synonym for *spectacular?*
  Ⓐ disappointing
  Ⓑ good
  Ⓒ ordinary
  Ⓓ wonderful

Synonyms and Antonyms in Context

Find the sentence with the same meaning.

1. Mom was *appalled* at my grades.
  Ⓐ Mom helped me with my grades.
  Ⓑ Mom did not like my grades.
  Ⓒ Mom was happy with my grades.
  Ⓓ Mom did not see my grades.

2. My baby sister is *bashful*.
  Ⓐ My baby sister is funny.
  Ⓑ My baby sister is crying
  Ⓒ My baby sister is shy.
  Ⓓ My baby sister is sleeping.

3. The family *contributed* to the bake sale.
  Ⓐ The family took part in the bake sale.
  Ⓑ The family did not go to the bake sale.
  Ⓒ The family got lost at the bake sale.
  Ⓓ The family set up for the bake sale.

4. The dog *disobeyed* its owner.
  Ⓐ The dog was bought by its owner.
  Ⓑ The dog listened to its owner.
  Ⓒ The dog pleased its owner.
  Ⓓ The dog did not listen to its owner.

5. Jamal is *crafty* when it comes to cooking.
  Ⓐ Jamal is a terrible cook.
  Ⓑ Jamal likes to cook.
  Ⓒ Jamal has some interesting cooking ideas.
  Ⓓ Jamal is hungry.

6. Mike could not *comprehend* the plans.
  Ⓐ Mike could not understand the plans.
  Ⓑ Mike understood the plans.
  Ⓒ Mike wrote the plans.
  Ⓓ Mike did not write the plans.

Find the sentence with the opposite meaning.

7. Jessie *devoured* the meal.
  Ⓐ Jessie did not eat everything.
  Ⓑ Jessie ate quickly.
  Ⓒ Jessie was hungry.
  Ⓓ Jessie made the meal.

8. The class *concentrated* on the lesson.
  Ⓐ The class started late.
  Ⓑ The class misunderstood the teacher.
  Ⓒ The class worked hard.
  Ⓓ The class did not listen well.

9. You will have to *interpret* the speech for Jill.
  Ⓐ Jill understood the speech.
  Ⓑ Jill did not understand the speech.
  Ⓒ Jill gave a speech.
  Ⓓ Jill listened carefully to the speech.

10. The teacher's stare was *disapproving*.
  Ⓐ The teacher stared.
  Ⓑ The teacher was looking in the wrong place.
  Ⓒ The teacher did not like what she saw.
  Ⓓ The teacher was pleased with what she saw.

Prefixes and Suffixes

Answer the questions below.

1. What is the prefix in the word *disgustingly?*
- Ⓐ dis-
- Ⓑ gust-
- Ⓒ ing-
- Ⓓ ly-

2. Which suffix means *a person who?*
- Ⓐ -ing
- Ⓑ -ly
- Ⓒ -ist
- Ⓓ -tion

3. Which does the prefix in *undisciplined* mean?
- Ⓐ large
- Ⓑ after
- Ⓒ before
- Ⓓ not

4. Which suffix can be added to the word *sell?*
- Ⓐ -ist
- Ⓑ -ly
- Ⓒ -ing
- Ⓓ -ive

5. Which prefix can be added to the word *impressed?*
- Ⓐ post-
- Ⓑ pre-
- Ⓒ dis-
- Ⓓ un-

6. Which suffix can be added to the word *perfection?*
- Ⓐ -ist
- Ⓑ -ly
- Ⓒ -ing
- Ⓓ -er

7. What does the word *reenter* mean?
- Ⓐ enter
- Ⓑ enter again
- Ⓒ in the process of entering
- Ⓓ a person who enters

8. What does the word *specialist* mean?
- Ⓐ the process of being special
- Ⓑ a person who is special at doing something
- Ⓒ a person who wants to be special
- Ⓓ a special event

9. Which prefix can be added to *attractive* to mean *not attractive?*
- Ⓐ post-
- Ⓑ re-
- Ⓒ un-
- Ⓓ dis-

10. Which suffix can be added to *retire* to mean *the state of being retired?*
- Ⓐ -ly
- Ⓑ -or
- Ⓒ -ist
- Ⓓ -ment

Similes, Metaphors, and Rhymes

Identify the sayings as simile, metaphor, rhyme, or none of the above.

1. *We are two peas in a pod.*
Ⓐ simile
Ⓑ metaphor
Ⓒ rhyme
Ⓓ none of the above

2. *The boat sailed through the water.*
Ⓐ simile
Ⓑ metaphor
Ⓒ rhyme
Ⓓ none of the above

3. *Her eyes were as bright as stars.*
Ⓐ simile
Ⓑ metaphor
Ⓒ rhyme
Ⓓ none of the above

4. *His room was messier than a pigpen.*
Ⓐ simile
Ⓑ metaphor
Ⓒ rhyme
Ⓓ none of the above

5. *See you later, alligator.*
Ⓐ simile
Ⓑ metaphor
Ⓒ rhyme
Ⓓ none of the above

6. *He is as proud as a peacock.*
Ⓐ simile
Ⓑ metaphor
Ⓒ rhyme
Ⓓ none of the above

7. *After a while, crocodile.*
Ⓐ simile
Ⓑ metaphor
Ⓒ rhyme
Ⓓ none of the above

8. *The lunchroom was a zoo.*
Ⓐ simile
Ⓑ metaphor
Ⓒ rhyme
Ⓓ none of the above

9. *If at first you don't succeed, try, try again.*
Ⓐ simile
Ⓑ metaphor
Ⓒ rhyme
Ⓓ none of the above

10. *The world is my stage.*
Ⓐ simile
Ⓑ metaphor
Ⓒ rhyme
Ⓓ none of the above

Punctuation

Answer the questions below.

1. Which sentence shows the correct end punctuation?
   Ⓐ What are you doing!
   Ⓑ What are you doing...
   Ⓒ What are you doing.
   Ⓓ What are you doing?

2. Which sentence shows incorrect punctuation?
   Ⓐ Come with me to my classroom.
   Ⓑ I have to show you something.
   Ⓒ "Wait," She said!
   Ⓓ "I have to go to lunch now."

3. Which sentence shows the correct punctuation?
   Ⓐ "Welcome to my parlor" said the spider to the fly.
   Ⓑ Welcome to my parlor, said the spider to the fly.
   Ⓒ "Welcome to my parlor," said the spider to the fly.
   Ⓓ "Welcome to my parlor," Said the Spider to the Fly.

4. Which sentence shows the correct use of commas?
   Ⓐ I like to play soccer, baseball, and basketball.
   Ⓑ I like to play soccer baseball and basketball.
   Ⓒ I like to play soccer baseball, and basketball.
   Ⓓ I like to play soccer, baseball and, basketball.

5. Which sentence is written correctly?
   Ⓐ The dog was born on June 22 2007.
   Ⓑ The dog was born on June, 22 2007.
   Ⓒ The dog was born on June, 22, 2007.
   Ⓓ The dog was born on June 22, 2007.

6. Which sentence is written correctly?
   Ⓐ are you my mother
   Ⓑ Are you my mother?
   Ⓒ Are you, my mother!
   Ⓓ Are you my mother.

7. What kind of punctuation belongs at the end of the sentence below?
   "Where are my shoes?" said Marco
   Ⓐ period
   Ⓑ exclamation point
   Ⓒ question mark
   Ⓓ quotation mark

8. Which part of the sentence below has an error?
   My fathers brother is my uncle.
   Ⓐ *fathers* should be *father's*
   Ⓑ *fathers* should be *fathers'*
   Ⓒ *brother* should be *brother's*
   Ⓓ *is* should be *are*

Capitalization

Answer the questions below.

1. Which word should **not** be capitalized in the sentence below?

   george moved to mexico in july.

   Ⓐ george
   Ⓑ moved
   Ⓒ mexico
   Ⓓ july

2. Which word should **not** be capitalized in the sentence below?

   My Friend lives on Spring Street with Luis.

   Ⓐ Friend
   Ⓑ Spring
   Ⓒ Street
   Ⓓ Luis

3. Which words should **not** be capitalized in a sentence?

   Ⓐ days of the week
   Ⓑ months
   Ⓒ names of people and places
   Ⓓ names of objects

4. Which words should be capitalized in a sentence?

   Ⓐ shaker road
   Ⓑ blue car
   Ⓒ cat
   Ⓓ tomato

5. Which sentence is written correctly?

   Ⓐ Tomorrow is friday the 13th.
   Ⓑ tomorrow is Friday the 13th.
   Ⓒ Tomorrow is Friday the 13th.
   Ⓓ tomorrow is friday the 13th.

6. Which sentence shows the correct capitalization?

   Ⓐ Jenna and Hubert live in miami.
   Ⓑ Jenna and hubert live in miami.
   Ⓒ jenna and hubert live in Miami.
   Ⓓ Jenna and Hubert live in Miami.

7. Which item should **not** be capitalized in a sentence?

   Ⓐ England
   Ⓑ San Francisco
   Ⓒ Monkey
   Ⓓ Tuesday

8. Which sentence shows the correct capitalization?

   Ⓐ The Barbecue is on Atlanta Street.
   Ⓑ The barbecue is on Atlanta Street.
   Ⓒ The barbecue is on Atlanta street.
   Ⓓ The barbecue is on atlanta Street.

9. Which sentence does **not** show the correct capitalization?

   Ⓐ I will go to France next Thursday.
   Ⓑ Dad will take me to the Airport.
   Ⓒ I will stay there until November.
   Ⓓ Then I will return to San Diego.

10. Which sentence is written correctly?

    Ⓐ Martha and Tam live on Juniper Avenue.
    Ⓑ Martha and Tam live on juniper Avenue.
    Ⓒ Martha and tam live on juniper Avenue.
    Ⓓ Martha and Tam live on Juniper avenue.

Plural Nouns

Choose the plural noun spelling of each noun below.

1. mouse
- Ⓐ mouses
- Ⓑ mous's
- Ⓒ mice
- Ⓓ mices

2. fox
- Ⓐ foxes
- Ⓑ foxes's
- Ⓒ foxs
- Ⓓ fox's

3. ski
- Ⓐ skies
- Ⓑ skys
- Ⓒ skees
- Ⓓ skis

4. boot
- Ⓐ boots
- Ⓑ bootes
- Ⓒ bootss
- Ⓓ bootz

5. beach
- Ⓐ beachs
- Ⓑ beaches
- Ⓒ beachees
- Ⓓ beach's

6. switch
- Ⓐ switch's
- Ⓑ switche's
- Ⓒ switches
- Ⓓ switchs

7. power
- Ⓐ poweres
- Ⓑ powers
- Ⓒ power's
- Ⓓ powere's

8. shelf
- Ⓐ shelves
- Ⓑ shelfs
- Ⓒ shelfes
- Ⓓ shelvs

9. bee
- Ⓐ bee's
- Ⓑ bee'es
- Ⓒ beees
- Ⓓ bees

10. wolf
- Ⓐ wolfs
- Ⓑ wolfes
- Ⓒ wolves
- Ⓓ wolf's

11. kiss
- Ⓐ kisss
- Ⓑ kiss's
- Ⓒ kisses
- Ⓓ kises

12. pony
- Ⓐ ponies
- Ⓑ ponys
- Ⓒ pony's
- Ⓓ pones

Multiple Meaning Words

Answer the questions below.

1. *The shelf is leaning at an angle.* What else does *angle* mean?
   - Ⓐ shape
   - Ⓑ a way of looking at something
   - Ⓒ a way of talking
   - Ⓓ strong

2. *I sign my name on the paper.* What else does *sign* mean?
   - Ⓐ to speak a language with your hands
   - Ⓑ a board that gives information
   - Ⓒ a way of telling that something will happen
   - Ⓓ all of the above

3. *I can handle the problem.* What else does *handle* mean?
   - Ⓐ a tool that opens a door
   - Ⓑ a tool for drinking
   - Ⓒ a way of running
   - Ⓓ a musical instrument

4. *I will run the meeting.* What else does *run* mean?
   - Ⓐ to crawl
   - Ⓑ to move quickly on foot
   - Ⓒ to meet with someone
   - Ⓓ to go shopping

5. *Flowers grow during the spring.* What else does *spring* mean?
   - Ⓐ a sudden jump
   - Ⓑ a spiral object that can be pressed or stretched
   - Ⓒ an underwater supply of water or oil
   - Ⓓ all of the above

6. *I was upset by your answer.* What else does *upset* mean?
   - Ⓐ to make again
   - Ⓑ to understand
   - Ⓒ to make a big change at the last minute
   - Ⓓ all of the above

7. *We rose to sing the "Star-Spangled Banner."* What else does *rose* mean?
   - Ⓐ a kind of plant
   - Ⓑ a kind of car
   - Ⓒ a kind of pencil
   - Ⓓ all of the above

8. *We follow the trail.* What else does *trail* mean?
   - Ⓐ to make a mistake
   - Ⓑ to move
   - Ⓒ to follow slowly
   - Ⓓ to impress

9. *A spark came from the outlet.* What else does *spark* mean?
   - Ⓐ to cook
   - Ⓑ to inspire
   - Ⓒ to talk to
   - Ⓓ to try

10. *They made a nice craft at school.* What else does *craft* mean?
    - Ⓐ an effort
    - Ⓑ a meal
    - Ⓒ a desire
    - Ⓓ a skill

Spelling

Answer the questions below.

1. Which word is spelled incorrectly?
- Ⓐ discover
- Ⓑ discrase
- Ⓒ disappear
- Ⓓ distrust

2. Which word is spelled correctly?
- Ⓐ towle
- Ⓑ littel
- Ⓒ special
- Ⓓ vowele

3. Which word is the correct spelling of a shape?
- Ⓐ tryangle
- Ⓑ rectangel
- Ⓒ circel
- Ⓓ square

4. Which word is the correct spelling of a kind of food?
- Ⓐ spagetti
- Ⓑ meatbals
- Ⓒ bread
- Ⓓ sause

5. Which word is spelled correctly?
- Ⓐ describe
- Ⓑ practise
- Ⓒ exercice
- Ⓓ cleen

6. Which word shows a day of the week spelled incorrectly?
- Ⓐ Monday
- Ⓑ Tuesday
- Ⓒ Wensday
- Ⓓ Thursday

7. Which word shows a kind of career spelled incorrectly?
- Ⓐ astrounaut
- Ⓑ surgeon
- Ⓒ ballerina
- Ⓓ teacher

8. Which word is **not** spelled correctly?
- Ⓐ giggle
- Ⓑ jingel
- Ⓒ jungle
- Ⓓ juggle

9. Which word is the incorrect spelling of a color?
- Ⓐ lavender
- Ⓑ purple
- Ⓒ vilot
- Ⓓ pink

10. Which word is spelled correctly?
- Ⓐ excitment
- Ⓑ movment
- Ⓒ statment
- Ⓓ treatment

Vocabulary

Choose the word that shows the meaning of each underlined word below.

1. small <u>fraction</u>
- Ⓐ state
- Ⓑ person
- Ⓒ part
- Ⓓ tiny

2. <u>annual</u> gift
- Ⓐ daily
- Ⓑ weekly
- Ⓒ monthly
- Ⓓ yearly

3. friendly <u>buddy</u>
- Ⓐ friend
- Ⓑ animal
- Ⓒ man
- Ⓓ woman

4. <u>conceal</u> a weapon
- Ⓐ carry
- Ⓑ hide
- Ⓒ use
- Ⓓ destroy

5. <u>embrace</u> a grandparent
- Ⓐ talk to
- Ⓑ look at
- Ⓒ hug
- Ⓓ kiss

6. <u>intelligent</u> dolphin
- Ⓐ large
- Ⓑ small
- Ⓒ friendly
- Ⓓ smart

7. <u>patient</u> person
- Ⓐ calm
- Ⓑ excited
- Ⓒ happy
- Ⓓ silly

8. good <u>pupil</u>
- Ⓐ friend
- Ⓑ sibling
- Ⓒ student
- Ⓓ teacher

9. <u>vast</u> desert
- Ⓐ hot
- Ⓑ dry
- Ⓒ good tasting
- Ⓓ large

10. <u>delicious</u> dessert
- Ⓐ hot
- Ⓑ dry
- Ⓒ good tasting
- Ⓓ large

11. warm <u>climate</u>
- Ⓐ storm
- Ⓑ weather
- Ⓒ sunny
- Ⓓ humidity

12. minor <u>accident</u>
- Ⓐ confusion
- Ⓑ chance
- Ⓒ risk
- Ⓓ mistake

Homophones

Fill in the blank with the best answer for each sentence below.

1. He gave her a nice _____ .
Ⓐ compliment
Ⓑ complement
Ⓒ complament
Ⓓ none of the above

2. You do not _____ me.
Ⓐ knead
Ⓑ kneed
Ⓒ need
Ⓓ none of the above

3. Let's read the _____ .
Ⓐ male
Ⓑ mail
Ⓒ mayl
Ⓓ none of the above

4. We _____ here in our boat.
Ⓐ rowed
Ⓑ road
Ⓒ rode
Ⓓ none of the above

5. You are not _____ in this room.
Ⓐ alloud
Ⓑ aloud
Ⓒ allowed
Ⓓ none of the above

6. We need some _____ for our recipe.
Ⓐ flour
Ⓑ flower
Ⓒ flowur
Ⓓ none of the above

7. I will be a _____ for Halloween.
Ⓐ whitch
Ⓑ which
Ⓒ witch
Ⓓ none of the above

8. The _____ ran away when it saw people.
Ⓐ dear
Ⓑ dere
Ⓒ deer
Ⓓ none of the above

9. You are the only person in _____ .
Ⓐ site
Ⓑ sigh
Ⓒ sighed
Ⓓ none of the above

10. I put milk in my _____ .
Ⓐ cereal
Ⓑ serial
Ⓒ see real
Ⓓ none of the above

11. We _____ our bikes.
Ⓐ petal
Ⓑ pedal
Ⓒ peddle
Ⓓ none of the above

12. Jorge won the gold _____ .
Ⓐ medal
Ⓑ metal
Ⓒ meddle
Ⓓ none of the above

Context Clues

Find the meaning of each underlined word.

1. Susie was <u>thrust</u> onto the field by the coach.
Ⓐ cheered
Ⓑ encouraged
Ⓒ pushed
Ⓓ invited

2. The children <u>swarm</u> around the birthday cake.
Ⓐ to move together in a group
Ⓑ to eat
Ⓒ to look
Ⓓ to discover

3. The drawer is filled with <u>valuable</u> jewelry.
Ⓐ pretty
Ⓑ handmade
Ⓒ bright
Ⓓ expensive

4. We will have to <u>postpone</u> the picnic.
Ⓐ schedule for an earlier time
Ⓑ schedule for a later time
Ⓒ celebrate
Ⓓ plan

5. I will <u>vow</u> never to lie to my parents again.
Ⓐ promise
Ⓑ cheat
Ⓒ lie
Ⓓ complain

6. She made a <u>remark</u> about his funny hat.
Ⓐ request
Ⓑ comment
Ⓒ problem
Ⓓ invitation

7. The storm caused <u>severe</u> damage to the house.
Ⓐ weak
Ⓑ serious
Ⓒ cold
Ⓓ hot

8. I can <u>assist</u> you with your homework.
Ⓐ invite
Ⓑ try
Ⓒ help
Ⓓ forget

9. My dad <u>commutes</u> to the city for work.
Ⓐ walks
Ⓑ swims
Ⓒ travels for lunch
Ⓓ travels between work and home

10. Marshall is caught in a <u>blizzard</u>.
Ⓐ rainbow
Ⓑ snowstorm
Ⓒ sunny day
Ⓓ cloudy day

11. We <u>ascend</u> the stairs to the roof.
Ⓐ go up
Ⓑ go down
Ⓒ walk fast
Ⓓ race

12. <u>Pardon</u> my messy room.
Ⓐ see
Ⓑ punish
Ⓒ explain
Ⓓ excuse

Combining Sentences

Choose the word that best combines the sentences.

1. Mark likes turkey. He likes wheat bread.
   - Ⓐ and
   - Ⓑ but
   - Ⓒ or
   - Ⓓ none of the above

2. Sara has art class. She will not be able to go because she is sick.
   - Ⓐ and
   - Ⓑ but
   - Ⓒ or
   - Ⓓ none of the above

3. Juan bought spinach for his mom. He does not like spinach.
   - Ⓐ and
   - Ⓑ but
   - Ⓒ or
   - Ⓓ none of the above

4. Finish your homework. Finish as much as possible.
   - Ⓐ and
   - Ⓑ but
   - Ⓒ or
   - Ⓓ none of the above

5. We are baking a cake. We are making cookies.
   - Ⓐ and
   - Ⓑ but
   - Ⓒ or
   - Ⓓ none of the above

6. Do you want to play? Should I play alone?
   - Ⓐ and
   - Ⓑ but
   - Ⓒ or
   - Ⓓ none of the above

7. I cannot read the sign. Because I don't have my glasses.
   - Ⓐ and
   - Ⓑ but
   - Ⓒ or
   - Ⓓ none of the above

8. Tell me everything about it. Don't leave anything out.
   - Ⓐ and
   - Ⓑ but
   - Ⓒ or
   - Ⓓ none of the above

9. You can have only the blue umbrella. You can have only the green umbrella.
   - Ⓐ and
   - Ⓑ but
   - Ⓒ or
   - Ⓓ none of the above

10. Read the book. When you are finished, tell me how it ends.
    - Ⓐ and
    - Ⓑ but
    - Ⓒ or
    - Ⓓ none of the above

Parts of Speech

Answer the questions below.

1. What part of speech is *circular?*
- Ⓐ noun
- Ⓑ verb
- Ⓒ adjective
- Ⓓ preposition

2. What part of speech is *atmosphere?*
- Ⓐ noun
- Ⓑ verb
- Ⓒ adjective
- Ⓓ preposition

3. What part of speech is *accident?*
- Ⓐ noun
- Ⓑ verb
- Ⓒ adjective
- Ⓓ preposition

4. What part of speech is *after?*
- Ⓐ noun
- Ⓑ verb
- Ⓒ adjective
- Ⓓ preposition

5. What part of speech is *adapt?*
- Ⓐ noun
- Ⓑ verb
- Ⓒ adjective
- Ⓓ preposition

6. What part of speech is *lazy?*
- Ⓐ noun
- Ⓑ verb
- Ⓒ adjective
- Ⓓ preposition

7. What is the preposition in the sentence below?

Lori put an extra egg into the cake.
- Ⓐ put
- Ⓑ extra
- Ⓒ into
- Ⓓ the

8. What is the adverb in the sentence below?

She spoke quietly to the teacher.
- Ⓐ she
- Ⓑ spoke
- Ⓒ quietly
- Ⓓ to

9. What is the pronoun in the sentence below?

David wants to help them.
- Ⓐ David
- Ⓑ wants
- Ⓒ to
- Ⓓ them

10. What is the article in the sentence below?

She ordered salad and a juice.
- Ⓐ she
- Ⓑ and
- Ⓒ a
- Ⓓ juice

Verb Tense

Answer the questions below.

1. What is the future tense of *argue?*
   - Ⓐ will argue
   - Ⓑ argue
   - Ⓒ argued
   - Ⓓ arguing

2. What is the past tense of *fly?*
   - Ⓐ flight
   - Ⓑ will fly
   - Ⓒ flyed
   - Ⓓ flew

3. What is the present tense of *drank?*
   - Ⓐ drunk
   - Ⓑ drinked
   - Ⓒ drink
   - Ⓓ will drink

4. What is the past tense of *assist?*
   - Ⓐ will assist
   - Ⓑ assists
   - Ⓒ assistant
   - Ⓓ assisted

5. Which sentence is written in the present tense?
   - Ⓐ I planted carrots every year.
   - Ⓑ I will plant carrots later this year.
   - Ⓒ I plant carrots every year.
   - Ⓓ I will plant carrots next Tuesday.

6. Which sentence is written in the future tense?
   - Ⓐ Did you pass me that bag of lemons?
   - Ⓑ Will you pass me that bag of lemons?
   - Ⓒ Where is that bag of lemons?
   - Ⓓ Can you pass me that bag of lemons?

7. Which sentence is written in the present tense?
   - Ⓐ Grandma is visiting our house.
   - Ⓑ Grandma will be visiting our house.
   - Ⓒ Grandma was going to visit our house.
   - Ⓓ Grandma visited our house.

8. Which sentence is **not** written in the future tense?
   - Ⓐ Will you be going to the dance with Tommy?
   - Ⓑ I will ask him to the dance myself.
   - Ⓒ You will be able to dance with him too.
   - Ⓓ Where is Tommy, anyway?

9. Which sentence is **not** written in the past tense?
   - Ⓐ We won the game.
   - Ⓑ Kari made a goal at the last minute.
   - Ⓒ We will buy her a slice of pizza.
   - Ⓓ We won the first game of the season.

10. Which sentence is **not** written in the present tense?
    - Ⓐ Tell me your name.
    - Ⓑ I know who you are.
    - Ⓒ You are friends with my cousin.
    - Ⓓ He told me your name is Mike.

Subject and Verb Agreement

Answer the questions below.

1. Complete the sentence below correctly.

Mack _____ his guitar back.

Ⓐ want

Ⓑ wants

Ⓒ will wants

Ⓓ will wanted

2. Which sentence is correct?

Ⓐ Let's walk the dog.

Ⓑ Let's walks the dog.

Ⓒ Let's walking the dog.

Ⓓ Let's walked the dog.

3. Which verb should be used in the sentence below?

Put on your mittens, it _____ cold outside.

Ⓐ be

Ⓑ are

Ⓒ is

Ⓓ were

4. Which subject should be used in the sentence below?

_____ buys a new tent.

Ⓐ The family

Ⓑ The children

Ⓒ The campers

Ⓓ Dad's

5. Which sentence is correct?

Ⓐ You must goes to the doctor.

Ⓑ You must go to the doctor.

Ⓒ You has to go to the doctor.

Ⓓ You had to goes to the doctor.

6. Which word correctly fills in the blank in the sentence below?

My teacher _____ in a marathon.

Ⓐ run

Ⓑ running

Ⓒ ran

Ⓓ runner

7. Which sentence is correct?

Ⓐ Abby did not makes her bed.

Ⓑ Abby did not made her bed.

Ⓒ Abby did not making her bed.

Ⓓ Abby did not make her bed.

8. Which subject should be used in the sentence below?

_____ sing in the school play.

Ⓐ We

Ⓑ She

Ⓒ He

Ⓓ Mom

9. Which sentence is correct?

Ⓐ The playground are open today.

Ⓑ The playground is open today.

Ⓒ The playgrounds is open today.

Ⓓ The playgrounds isn't open today.

10. Which subject should be used in the sentence below?

_____ bakes the best cookies in the world.

Ⓐ Grandma

Ⓑ Grandma and Grandpa

Ⓒ Mom and Dad

Ⓓ I

Irregular Verbs

Choose the past tense of each verb.

1. rise
- Ⓐ rised
- Ⓑ rose
- Ⓒ rosed
- Ⓓ rises

2. build
- Ⓐ built
- Ⓑ builted
- Ⓒ builded
- Ⓓ buildd

3. buy
- Ⓐ buyed
- Ⓑ buyded
- Ⓒ bought
- Ⓓ boughted

4. cling
- Ⓐ clinged
- Ⓑ cling
- Ⓒ clunged
- Ⓓ clung

5. get
- Ⓐ got
- Ⓑ gotted
- Ⓒ getted
- Ⓓ getd

6. kneel
- Ⓐ kneelted
- Ⓑ kneeld
- Ⓒ knelt
- Ⓓ knelted

7. mistake
- Ⓐ mistook
- Ⓑ mistooked
- Ⓒ mistaked
- Ⓓ mistakd

8. speak
- Ⓐ speaked
- Ⓑ spoke
- Ⓒ spooked
- Ⓓ spoked

9. oversleep
- Ⓐ oversleeped
- Ⓑ overslepted
- Ⓒ overslept
- Ⓓ oversleepd

10. repay
- Ⓐ repayed
- Ⓑ repayd
- Ⓒ repaid
- Ⓓ repaided

11. bring
- Ⓐ brang
- Ⓑ broughted
- Ⓒ bringed
- Ⓓ brought

12. hit
- Ⓐ hited
- Ⓑ hit
- Ⓒ hitted
- Ⓓ hid

Editing and Proofreading

Answer the questions below.

1. How can the sentence below be corrected?

"Come over here" said the Man.

Ⓐ "Come over here," said the Man.

Ⓑ "Come over here" said the man.

Ⓒ "Come over here." said the man.

Ⓓ "Come over here," said the man.

2. How can the sentence below be corrected?

My family gotted me a dog for my Birthday.

Ⓐ My family got me a dog for my Birthday.

Ⓑ My family gotted me a dog for my birthday.

Ⓒ My family got me a dog for my birthday.

Ⓓ My family gots me a dog for my birthday.

3. How can the sentence below be corrected?

i was late for the movie?

Ⓐ i was late for the movie.

Ⓑ I was late for the Movie?

Ⓒ I was late for the movie.

Ⓓ I was late for the movie?

4. How can the sentence below be corrected?

Lets get ice cream after the game on Saturday.

Ⓐ Let's get ice cream after the game on Saturday.

Ⓑ Lets get Ice Cream after the game on Saturday.

Ⓒ Let's get ice cream after the game on saturday.

Ⓓ Let's gets ice cream after the game on Saturday.

5. How can the sentence below be corrected?

Where did I put my coat!

Ⓐ Where did i put my coat!

Ⓑ Where did I put my Coat.

Ⓒ Where did I put my coat.

Ⓓ Where did I put my coat?

6. How can the sentence below be corrected?

"You are my best friend, said Rabbit."

Ⓐ "You are my best friend said Rabbit.

Ⓑ "You are my best friend," said Rabbit.

Ⓒ "You are my best friend said Rabbit."

Ⓓ "You are my best friend" said Rabbit.

7. Which word shows a spelling error?

Ⓐ correct

Ⓑ propor

Ⓒ interesting

Ⓓ all of the above

8. Which sentence below has an error?

Ⓐ Judy fell asleep in my sleeping bag.

Ⓑ I bought the new bag in march.

Ⓒ This is the first time we're using it.

Ⓓ I will use it again on Labor Day.

Section 3: Test

Read the passages and answer the questions.

The Common Cold

Just about everyone has had a cold at one time or another. The common cold can be caused by a number of viruses. When a virus that causes a cold gets into your body, it can cause many symptoms. You might have a runny nose, a sneeze, a cough, or a headache.

Sometimes a cold can reach the cells that line your lungs. When this happens, you may cough a lot. There are some medicines that can help relieve the symptoms of a cold. However, there is no cure for a cold. Your body must fight the illness on its own. You should see a doctor if you have a fever for more than a few days. Most colds do not cause fevers, so a fever can often be a sign of a more serious illness, such as an ear infection, pneumonia, or bronchitis.

1. What causes a common cold?
Ⓐ a cough
Ⓑ a virus
Ⓒ a sneeze
Ⓓ an ear infection

2. Which is **not** usually a symptom of a cold?
Ⓐ runny nose
Ⓑ sneeze
Ⓒ cough
Ⓓ fever

3. What makes people cough from a cold?
Ⓐ The cold reaches the person's nose.
Ⓑ The cold reaches the person's lungs.
Ⓒ The cold reaches the person's stomach.
Ⓓ A cough is not a symptom of a cold.

4. What is the **best** cure for a cold?
Ⓐ medicine
Ⓑ exercise
Ⓒ fever
Ⓓ There is no cure for the cold.

5. What are some illnesses that are more serious than a cold?
Ⓐ bronchitis
Ⓑ ear infection
Ⓒ pneumonia
Ⓓ all of the above

6. When should you see a doctor for a cold?
Ⓐ every time you have a cold
Ⓑ if you have a fever for one day
Ⓒ if you have a fever for several days
Ⓓ if you cough at all

My Cold

My name is Lucy, and today is the worst day of my life. I just came down with a cold. This morning I felt fine, then just as I was getting off the school bus and walking into the school, I had a sneezing attack. I must have sneezed seven or eight times in a row. The other kids moved away from me because I sounded so sick. The cold hit me faster than a curveball on the playing field.

At lunchtime I couldn't eat. I just felt too miserable. So I went to the nurse and she called my mom to pick me up. Now I'm just lying in my bed while my mom makes me some soup. She says that nothing cures a cold like her homemade chicken soup. I take a few mouthfuls, but mostly I just want to crawl under the covers and sleep!

7. Who is the main character of the story?
Ⓐ Lucy
Ⓑ the bus driver
Ⓒ the school nurse
Ⓓ Lucy's mom

8. Why doesn't Lucy feel good?
Ⓐ She has a stomachache.
Ⓑ She has a fever.
Ⓒ She has a cold.
Ⓓ She hurt her leg.

9. Who called Lucy's mom to pick her up from school?
Ⓐ Lucy
Ⓑ the school nurse
Ⓒ the principal
Ⓓ Lucy's teacher

10. What is the setting of the story?
Ⓐ Lucy's home, in the future
Ⓑ Lucy's home and school, in the present day
Ⓒ Lucy's school, in the future
Ⓓ Lucy's home, in the past

11. How does this passage compare to the one called "The Common Cold?"
Ⓐ They are both about Lucy.
Ⓑ They are both nonfiction.
Ⓒ They are both fiction.
Ⓓ They are both about colds.

12. What is the first thing that Lucy does in the story?
Ⓐ She gets on the school bus.
Ⓑ She starts to sneeze.
Ⓒ She cannot eat her lunch.
Ⓓ She eats her mom's soup.

Answer the questions below.

13. What is a synonym for *collected*?
- Ⓐ gather
- Ⓑ gathered
- Ⓒ together
- Ⓓ apart

14. Which sentence uses the word *exhausted* correctly?
- Ⓐ He had exhausted the dinner plate.
- Ⓑ He had exhausted the soccer ball.
- Ⓒ He had exhausted the bicycle.
- Ⓓ He had exhausted the dog.

15. Find the sentence with the opposite meaning of the one below.

The boys were opposed to the idea of cooking dinner.
- Ⓐ The boys did not like the idea of cooking dinner.
- Ⓑ The boys liked the idea of cooking dinner.
- Ⓒ The boys did not know how to cook dinner.
- Ⓓ The boys knew just what they wanted to cook for dinner.

16. Fill in the blank with the verb that agrees with the subject in the sentence below.

Laurie _____ to the parade with her sister.
- Ⓐ go
- Ⓑ to go
- Ⓒ went
- Ⓓ to went

17. Which prefix means *after*?
- Ⓐ pre-
- Ⓑ post-
- Ⓒ re-
- Ⓓ un-

18. Which word is spelled incorrectly?
- Ⓐ impressive
- Ⓑ programe
- Ⓒ battle
- Ⓓ difficult

19. What is the meaning of the underlined word below?

complicated directions
- Ⓐ difficult
- Ⓑ easy
- Ⓒ correct
- Ⓓ incorrect

20. What part of speech is the underlined word in the sentence below?

Soon we will encounter a storm.
- Ⓐ verb
- Ⓑ noun
- Ⓒ adjective
- Ⓓ preposition

21. What is the plural of *trick?*
  Ⓐ trickses
  Ⓑ trixes
  Ⓒ tricks
  Ⓓ trix

22. Which sentence is correct?
  Ⓐ My brother was born on memorial day.
  Ⓑ My Brother was born on memorial day.
  Ⓒ My brother was born on Memorial day.
  Ⓓ My brother was born on Memorial Day.

23. Which sentence is correct?
  Ⓐ "Lets go to the mall," I said.
  Ⓑ "Let's go to the mall," I said.
  Ⓒ "Let's go to the mall" I said.
  Ⓓ "Let's go to the mall, I said.

24. What is the past tense of the verb *catch?*
  Ⓐ catched
  Ⓑ catchd
  Ⓒ caught
  Ⓓ caughted

25. Fill in the blank in the sentence below with the correct verb.
  The camel _____ through the desert.
  Ⓐ walked
  Ⓑ walkd
  Ⓒ will walked
  Ⓓ will walks

26. Which word is spelled correctly?
  Ⓐ anticipate
  Ⓑ britely
  Ⓒ simplefy
  Ⓓ arranje

27. What suffix can be added to *enjoy* to show the action happening right now?
  Ⓐ -ment
  Ⓑ -ing
  Ⓒ -ly
  Ⓓ -ful

28. Which word means the opposite of *discouraged?*
  Ⓐ discourage
  Ⓑ courage
  Ⓒ encourage
  Ⓓ encouraged

29. What does *exchange* mean in the sentence below?
  We should go to the store to exchange that shirt for a larger size.
  Ⓐ to buy something
  Ⓑ to change one thing for another
  Ⓒ to return something
  Ⓓ to go shopping

30. How can the sentence below be corrected?
  We cant swim if the Weather is Cold.
  Ⓐ We can't swim if the weather is cold.
  Ⓑ We can't swim if the weather is Cold.
  Ⓒ We can't swim if the Weather is cold.
  Ⓓ We cant swim if the weather is cold.

Section 4: Number Sense

Reading and Writing Whole Numbers

Solve the problems below.

1. Which number shows five million, four hundred thousand and twelve?
- Ⓐ 5,000,412
- Ⓑ 5,400,012
- Ⓒ 5,412,000
- Ⓓ 5,412,012

2. Which number shows one million, three hundred eighty-one thousand, five hundred and eleven?
- Ⓐ 1,381,511
- Ⓑ 1,380,501
- Ⓒ 1,318,501
- Ⓓ 138,511

3. Which number shows 3,001,001?
- Ⓐ three million, one hundred thousand and one
- Ⓑ three million, ten thousand and one
- Ⓒ three million, one thousand and one
- Ⓓ three million and one

4. Which number shows 9,812,452?
- Ⓐ nine million, eight hundred twelve and four hundred fifty-two
- Ⓑ nine million, eighty-one thousand, four hundred fifty-two
- Ⓒ nine million, eight hundred two, four hundred two
- Ⓓ nine million, eight hundred twelve thousand, four hundred fifty-two

5. Which number shows eleven million?
- Ⓐ 11,000
- Ⓑ 1,100,000
- Ⓒ 11,000,000
- Ⓓ 11,000,011

6. Which number shows eighty-five thousand, twenty-one?
- Ⓐ 8,5210
- Ⓑ 85,021
- Ⓒ 85,210
- Ⓓ 8,500,000

7. Which number shows two hundred fifty thousand and eight?
- Ⓐ 250,008
- Ⓑ 250,800
- Ⓒ 2,050,008
- Ⓓ 2,500,008

8. Which number shows 8,392,000?
- Ⓐ eight million, three hundred ninety-two thousand
- Ⓑ eight million, three hundred twenty-nine thousand
- Ⓒ eighty-three million, ninety-two thousand
- Ⓓ eighty-three thousand, ninety-two

Ordering and Comparing Mixed Decimals

Solve the problems below.

1. Put these numbers in order from least to greatest: 85.29, 91.34, 73.20, 85.92
- Ⓐ 73.20, 85.29, 91.34, 85.92
- Ⓑ 91.34, 85.92, 85.29, 73.20
- Ⓒ 73.20, 85.29, 85.92, 91.34
- Ⓓ 73.20, 85.92, 85.29, 91.34

2. Which number sentence is true?
- Ⓐ 800.1 < 800.10
- Ⓑ 913.21 < 829.44
- Ⓒ 1.03 > 1.30
- Ⓓ 90.7 > 90.0

3. Which numbers are in order from least to greatest?
- Ⓐ 1.01, 1.001, 1.101, 1.0001
- Ⓑ 1.0001, 1.001, 1.01, 1.101
- Ⓒ 1.101, 1.0001, 1.001, 1.01
- Ⓓ 1.01, 1.001, 1.0001, 1.101

4. Which numbers are in order from greatest to least?
- Ⓐ 98.46, 88.11, 66.64, 21.00
- Ⓑ 98.46, 66.64, 21.00, 88.11
- Ⓒ 21.00, 88.11, 66.64, 98.46
- Ⓓ 21.00, 66.64, 88.11, 98.46

5. Which number sentence is true?
- Ⓐ 9.00 > 9.10
- Ⓑ 9.23 < 9.32
- Ⓒ 9.01 > 9.10
- Ⓓ 9.38 < 9.03

6. Which number is greater than 89.1?
- Ⓐ 89.00
- Ⓑ 89.01
- Ⓒ 89.10
- Ⓓ 89.11

7. Which number is less than 30.05?
- Ⓐ 30.04
- Ⓑ 30.05
- Ⓒ 30.06
- Ⓓ 30.50

8. Which number sentence is true?
- Ⓐ 12.34 > 12.43
- Ⓑ 15.29 > 15.92
- Ⓒ 83.11 < 83.12
- Ⓓ 99.10 < 99.01

9. Which number has the least value?
- Ⓐ 3.20
- Ⓑ 3.11
- Ⓒ 3.10
- Ⓓ 3.01

10. Which number has the greatest value?
- Ⓐ 7.98
- Ⓑ 7.35
- Ⓒ 7.99
- Ⓓ 7.09

Operations with Whole Numbers

Solve the problems below.

1. 7,002 + 522 =
- Ⓐ 7,524
- Ⓑ 7,542
- Ⓒ 7,552
- Ⓓ 7,554

2. 8,100 − 6,832 =
- Ⓐ 1,368
- Ⓑ 1,345
- Ⓒ 1,268
- Ⓓ 1,248

3. 81 × 7 =
- Ⓐ 657
- Ⓑ 567
- Ⓒ 557
- Ⓓ 546

4. 260 ÷ 5 =
- Ⓐ 31
- Ⓑ 32
- Ⓒ 51
- Ⓓ 52

5. 87,429 + 56,488 =
- Ⓐ 132,654
- Ⓑ 134,917
- Ⓒ 143,917
- Ⓓ 143,971

6. 66 × 9 =
- Ⓐ 594
- Ⓑ 584
- Ⓒ 583
- Ⓓ 514

7. 887 − 566 =
- Ⓐ 322
- Ⓑ 321
- Ⓒ 231
- Ⓓ 221

8. 976 ÷ 3 =
- Ⓐ 325
- Ⓑ 325R1
- Ⓒ 325R2
- Ⓓ 326

9. 8,442 × 70 =
- Ⓐ 599,564
- Ⓑ 590,994
- Ⓒ 590,940
- Ⓓ 509,940

10. 6,755 + 564 =
- Ⓐ 7,319
- Ⓑ 7,139
- Ⓒ 7,239
- Ⓓ 7,299

11. 1,981 + 1,968 =
- Ⓐ 3,499
- Ⓑ 4,294
- Ⓒ 2,949
- Ⓓ 3,949

12. 37 × 24 =
- Ⓐ 788
- Ⓑ 888
- Ⓒ 988
- Ⓓ 88

Operations with Decimals

Solve the problems below.

1. 678.54 + 8.23 =
Ⓐ 668.77
Ⓑ 686.77
Ⓒ 745.22
Ⓓ 775.22

2. 82.33 − 1.39 =
Ⓐ 80.94
Ⓑ 81.94
Ⓒ 81.49
Ⓓ 82.63

3. 85.5 ÷ 5 =
Ⓐ 16.1
Ⓑ 16.5
Ⓒ 17.1
Ⓓ 17.5

4. 97.5 × 5.6 =
Ⓐ 564
Ⓑ 546
Ⓒ 534
Ⓓ 536

5. 53.08 + 3.2 =
Ⓐ 56.02
Ⓑ 56.22
Ⓒ 56.25
Ⓓ 56.28

6. 829.7 − 39.4 =
Ⓐ 790.03
Ⓑ 790.3
Ⓒ 790.5
Ⓓ 790.7

7. 92.00 × 2.3 =
Ⓐ 211.6
Ⓑ 211.3
Ⓒ 211.1
Ⓓ 210.6

8. 75.96 ÷ 2 =
Ⓐ 39.89
Ⓑ 38.98
Ⓒ 37.98
Ⓓ 37.89

9. 78.34 − 62.99 =
Ⓐ 14.35
Ⓑ 14.53
Ⓒ 15.53
Ⓓ 15.35

10. 822.34 + 342.11 =
Ⓐ 1,466.65
Ⓑ 1,456.45
Ⓒ 1,164.45
Ⓓ 1,146.54

11. 642.17 + 647.2 =
Ⓐ 1,289.37
Ⓑ 1,829.73
Ⓒ 1,281.19
Ⓓ 1,289.19

12. 385.8 + 1.77 =
Ⓐ 862.788
Ⓑ 682.866
Ⓒ 682.85
Ⓓ 386.85

Word Problems

Solve the problems below.

1. Maggie buys 9 dozen eggs for the school bake sale. There are 12 eggs in one dozen. How many eggs did Maggie buy?
- Ⓐ 98
- Ⓑ 108
- Ⓒ 117
- Ⓓ 120

2. Deshawn reads a 627-page book. Greg reads a 539-page book. How many pages do the boys read in all?
- Ⓐ 1,043
- Ⓑ 1,066
- Ⓒ 1,156
- Ⓓ 1,166

3. Karie has 324 stamps. She uses 160. How many stamps does she have left?
- Ⓐ 156
- Ⓑ 160
- Ⓒ 164
- Ⓓ 166

4. Mark has 104 popsicle sticks. He gives an equal number of sticks to 4 friends. How many sticks does each friend get?
- Ⓐ 12
- Ⓑ 20
- Ⓒ 25
- Ⓓ 26

5. Miguel runs 2 miles every day. If he runs this for 30 days, how many miles will he have run altogether?
- Ⓐ 32
- Ⓑ 28
- Ⓒ 60
- Ⓓ 56

6. Mario wants to buy pizza for his party. Each pizza has 8 slices and there will be 24 people at the party. How many pizzas does he have to buy for each person to get 2 slices?
- Ⓐ 16
- Ⓑ 6
- Ⓒ 24
- Ⓓ 48

Word Problems with Money

Solve the problems below.

1. Mr. Lee buys grocery items for $3.25, $2.98, $2.10, and $4.29 each. How much does he spend in all?
Ⓐ $12.62
Ⓑ $12.26
Ⓒ $12.16
Ⓓ $11.98

2. Karen has $36.22 in her piggy bank. She splits the money evenly between her two sisters. How much does each sister get?
Ⓐ $17.98
Ⓑ $18.01
Ⓒ $18.11
Ⓓ $18.23

3. The store sells apples for $.32 each. Donnie buys 8 apples. How much does he pay?
Ⓐ $2.36
Ⓑ $2.56
Ⓒ $2.65
Ⓓ $2.76

4. Tara spends $17.44 at the store. She pays with a $20 bill. How much change does she get back?
Ⓐ $1.56
Ⓑ $1.85
Ⓒ $2.45
Ⓓ $2.56

5. Ed sold $126.75 worth of candy for his school fundraiser. Each box of candy costs $3.25. How many boxes did he sell?
Ⓐ 25
Ⓑ 29
Ⓒ 39
Ⓓ 411

6. Marlene buys 12 cupcakes at $1.75 each. She gets $4 back in change. How much did she pay with?
Ⓐ $25
Ⓑ $21
Ⓒ $30
Ⓓ $50

Fraction Concepts

Solve the problems below.

1. Which fraction equals .5?

(A) $\frac{4}{4}$

(B) $\frac{3}{4}$

(C) $\frac{1}{2}$

(D) $\frac{1}{4}$

2. Which fraction is largest?

(A) $\frac{1}{6}$

(B) $\frac{1}{10}$

(C) $\frac{1}{15}$

(D) $\frac{1}{100}$

3. Which fraction is smallest?

(A) $\frac{2}{4}$

(B) $\frac{2}{8}$

(C) $\frac{2}{12}$

(D) $\frac{2}{20}$

4. What fraction does the picture show?

(A) $\frac{1}{4}$

(B) $\frac{2}{7}$

(C) $\frac{2}{10}$

(D) $\frac{3}{9}$

5. What fraction does the picture show?

(A) $\frac{3}{5}$

(B) $\frac{3}{6}$

(C) $\frac{3}{10}$

(D) $\frac{3}{12}$

6. Which fraction equals 0?

(A) $\frac{0}{7}$

(B) $\frac{1}{7}$

(C) $\frac{2}{7}$

(D) $\frac{3}{7}$

7. Which fraction equals 1?

(A) $\frac{0}{2}$

(B) $\frac{1}{2}$

(C) $\frac{2}{2}$

(D) $\frac{2}{1}$

8. Which fraction equals .4?

(A) $\frac{4}{8}$

(B) $\frac{2}{4}$

(C) $\frac{1}{4}$

(D) $\frac{4}{10}$

9. Which fraction equals .75?

(A) $\frac{4}{4}$

(B) $\frac{3}{4}$

(C) $\frac{2}{4}$

(D) $\frac{1}{4}$

10. Which fraction equals .8?

(A) $\frac{1}{5}$

(B) $\frac{2}{5}$

(C) $\frac{4}{5}$

(D) $\frac{4}{10}$

Operations with Fractions

Solve the problems below.

1. $\frac{3}{6} + \frac{3}{6} =$

  Ⓐ $\frac{1}{2}$

  Ⓑ $\frac{4}{5}$

  Ⓒ $\frac{5}{6}$

  Ⓓ $\frac{6}{6}$

2. $\frac{2}{5} + \frac{1}{5} =$

  Ⓐ $\frac{1}{10}$

  Ⓑ $\frac{1}{5}$

  Ⓒ $\frac{3}{10}$

  Ⓓ $\frac{3}{5}$

3. $\frac{4}{8} + \frac{3}{8} =$

  Ⓐ $\frac{8}{8}$

  Ⓑ $\frac{7}{8}$

  Ⓒ $\frac{5}{8}$

  Ⓓ $\frac{3}{8}$

4. $\frac{4}{5} - \frac{2}{5} =$

  Ⓐ $\frac{3}{5}$

  Ⓑ $\frac{2}{5}$

  Ⓒ $\frac{1}{5}$

  Ⓓ $\frac{0}{5}$

5. $\frac{4}{5} \times \frac{3}{5} =$

  Ⓐ $\frac{12}{5}$

  Ⓑ $\frac{7}{5}$

  Ⓒ $\frac{12}{25}$

  Ⓓ $\frac{7}{25}$

6. $\frac{1}{3} \times \frac{2}{3} =$

  Ⓐ $\frac{2}{9}$

  Ⓑ $\frac{3}{9}$

  Ⓒ $\frac{4}{9}$

  Ⓓ $\frac{5}{9}$

7. Which number sentence shows $\frac{1}{4}$?

  Ⓐ $\frac{1}{4} + \frac{2}{4}$

  Ⓑ $\frac{3}{4} - \frac{2}{4}$

  Ⓒ $\frac{3}{4} - \frac{1}{4}$

  Ⓓ $\frac{2}{4} + \frac{3}{4}$

8. Which number sentence shows $\frac{5}{6}$?

  Ⓐ $\frac{6}{6} - \frac{4}{6}$

  Ⓑ $\frac{5}{6} - \frac{3}{6}$

  Ⓒ $\frac{2}{6} + \frac{3}{6}$

  Ⓓ $\frac{1}{6} + \frac{3}{6}$

9. Which number sentence shows $\frac{1}{10}$?

  Ⓐ $\frac{1}{5} \times \frac{1}{2}$

  Ⓑ $\frac{1}{5} \times \frac{3}{5}$

  Ⓒ $\frac{1}{5} + \frac{1}{2}$

  Ⓓ $\frac{1}{5} - \frac{1}{2}$

10. Which number sentence shows $\frac{3}{8}$?

  Ⓐ $\frac{3}{8} - \frac{1}{8}$

  Ⓑ $\frac{4}{8} \times \frac{1}{8}$

  Ⓒ $\frac{4}{8} + \frac{1}{8}$

  Ⓓ $\frac{4}{8} - \frac{1}{8}$

Section 5: Algebra and Functions

Number Patterns

Solve the problems below.

1. What is the missing number in this pattern?

14, 21, _____, 35, 42

Ⓐ 26
Ⓑ 28
Ⓒ 29
Ⓓ 32

2. What are the next two numbers in this pattern?

4,228, 4,230, 4,232, _____, _____

Ⓐ 4,232, 4,234
Ⓑ 4,233, 4,234
Ⓒ 4,234, 4,235
Ⓓ 4,234, 4,236

3. Which number sentence fits in this pattern?

8 × 2, 8 × 4, 8 × 6, 8 × 8, _____

Ⓐ 8 × 9
Ⓑ 8 × 8
Ⓒ 8 × 10
Ⓓ 8 × 12

4. What is the rule of this number pattern?

15, 20, 25, 30, 35

Ⓐ multiply by 5
Ⓑ multiply by 15
Ⓒ add 15
Ⓓ add 5

5. What is the rule of this number pattern?

7, 11, 15, 19, 23

Ⓐ add 3
Ⓑ multiply by 3
Ⓒ add 4
Ⓓ multiply by 4

6. What number comes next in this pattern?

5, 10, 20, 40, 80, _____

Ⓐ 180
Ⓑ 160
Ⓒ 120
Ⓓ 100

7. What is the missing number in this pattern?

7, 21, _____, 189, 567

Ⓐ 56
Ⓑ 61
Ⓒ 63
Ⓓ 67

8. What is the rule of this number pattern?

4, 12, 36, 108, 324

Ⓐ add 3
Ⓑ multiply by 3
Ⓒ add 8
Ⓓ multiply by 8

Choosing the Operation

Choose the operation that completes each number sentence.

1. 8,499 _____ 5,221 = 3,278
- Ⓐ +
- Ⓑ −
- Ⓒ ×
- Ⓓ ÷

2. 60 _____ 6 = 360
- Ⓐ +
- Ⓑ −
- Ⓒ ×
- Ⓓ ÷

3. 8,990 _____ 2,900 = 11,890
- Ⓐ +
- Ⓑ −
- Ⓒ ×
- Ⓓ ÷

4. 448 _____ 8 = 56
- Ⓐ +
- Ⓑ −
- Ⓒ ×
- Ⓓ ÷

5. 56.88 _____ 36.5 = 93.38
- Ⓐ +
- Ⓑ −
- Ⓒ ×
- Ⓓ ÷

6. 862.33 _____ 256.4 = 605.93
- Ⓐ +
- Ⓑ −
- Ⓒ ×
- Ⓓ ÷

7. 25.8 _____ 4.8 = 123.84
- Ⓐ +
- Ⓑ −
- Ⓒ ×
- Ⓓ ÷

8. 654.2 _____ 63.7 = 590.5
- Ⓐ +
- Ⓑ −
- Ⓒ ×
- Ⓓ ÷

9. 108.99 _____ 4 = 435.96
- Ⓐ +
- Ⓑ −
- Ⓒ ×
- Ⓓ ÷

10. 892.61 _____ 356.01 = 1,248.62
- Ⓐ +
- Ⓑ −
- Ⓒ ×
- Ⓓ ÷

Properties

Solve the problems below.

1. Which shows the identity property of division?
- Ⓐ $7 \div 1 = 7$
- Ⓑ $7 \div 7 = 1$
- Ⓒ $7 \div 0 = 0$
- Ⓓ $7 \div 7 = 0$

2. Which shows the associative property of multiplication?
- Ⓐ $4 \times (1 \times 6) = (4 \times 1) \times 6$
- Ⓑ $7 - (4 \times 2) = 2 \times (4 \times 7)$
- Ⓒ $5 + (2 \times 3) = 2 + (5 \times 3)$
- Ⓓ $9 + (6 \div 3) = 3 + (9 \div 6)$

3. What property does the number sentence below show?

$108 + 0 = 108$
- Ⓐ commutative property
- Ⓑ associative property
- Ⓒ distributive property
- Ⓓ identity property

4. What property does the number sentence below show?

$3 \times (8 - 2) = (3 \times 8) - (3 \times 2)$
- Ⓐ commutative property
- Ⓑ associative property
- Ⓒ distributive property
- Ⓓ identity property

5. Which shows the distributive property of multiplication?
- Ⓐ $9 \times (2 + 6) = 9 \times 2 \times 6$
- Ⓑ $9 \times (2 + 6) = (9 \times 2) \times (9 \times 6)$
- Ⓒ $9 \times (2 + 6) = (9 \times 2) + (9 \times 6)$
- Ⓓ $9 \times (2 + 6) = (9 + 2) + (9 \times 6)$

6. $(2 \times 5) \times 6 =$
- Ⓐ $(2 \times 5) + 6$
- Ⓑ $2 \times (5 \times 6)$
- Ⓒ $(2 + 5) + 6$
- Ⓓ $2 + (5 \times 6)$

7. $12 \times 4 \times 22 =$
- Ⓐ 12×22
- Ⓑ $22 \times 4 \times 12$
- Ⓒ $22 \times 4 + 12$
- Ⓓ $4 + 12 + 22$

8. What property does the number sentence below show?

$(14 + 3) + 10 = 14 + (3 + 10)$
- Ⓐ commutative property
- Ⓑ associative property
- Ⓒ distributive property
- Ⓓ identity property

9. What property does the number sentence below show?

$0 - 0 = 0$
- Ⓐ commutative property
- Ⓑ associative property
- Ⓒ distributive property
- Ⓓ identity property

10. What property does the number sentence below show?

$9 (8 - 3) = (9 \times 8) - (9 \times 3)$
- Ⓐ commutative property
- Ⓑ associative property
- Ⓒ distributive property
- Ⓓ identity property

Functions

Use the function table to answer questions 1–4.

3	5	7	9	11
24	40	56	72	?

1. What is the missing number in the function table?

Ⓐ 11

Ⓑ 88

Ⓒ 99

Ⓓ 110

2. What is the rule of the function table?

Ⓐ add 8

Ⓑ multiply by 8

Ⓒ add 11

Ⓓ multiply by 11

3. Which number sentence shows the second column of the table?

Ⓐ $3 + 8 = 24$

Ⓑ $3 \times 7 = 24$

Ⓒ $5 \times 8 = 40$

Ⓓ $40 \div 8 = 5$

4. Which column shows $7 \times a = 56$?

Ⓐ column 1

Ⓑ column 2

Ⓒ column 3

Ⓓ column 4

Use the function table to answer questions 5–8.

45	36	27	?	9
15	12	9	6	3

5. What is the value of the missing number?

Ⓐ 18

Ⓑ 20

Ⓒ 21

Ⓓ 32

6. What is the rule of the function table?

Ⓐ divide by 5

Ⓑ divide by 3

Ⓒ multiply by 3

Ⓓ multiply by 5

7. Which column shows $36 \div$ ___ $= 12$?

Ⓐ column 1

Ⓑ column 2

Ⓒ column 3

Ⓓ column 4

8. Which number sentence can be used to show the third column of the table?

Ⓐ $9 \times$ ___ $= 27$

Ⓑ ___ $+ 9 = 27$

Ⓒ $27 -$ ___ $= 9$

Ⓓ $27 \div 9 =$ ___

Finding the Variable

Solve the problems below.

1. $9,826 - y = 256$
- Ⓐ 674
- Ⓑ 3,199
- Ⓒ 9,570
- Ⓓ 9,750

2. $89 \times y = 178$
- Ⓐ 1
- Ⓑ 2
- Ⓒ 3
- Ⓓ 4

3. $900 + y = 900$
- Ⓐ 0
- Ⓑ 1
- Ⓒ 450
- Ⓓ 900

4. $87.5 \div y = 43.75$
- Ⓐ 0
- Ⓑ 1
- Ⓒ 2
- Ⓓ 3

5. $722.93 + y = 812.15$
- Ⓐ 94.17
- Ⓑ 92.19
- Ⓒ 89.45
- Ⓓ 89.22

6. $84 \times y = 420$
- Ⓐ 3
- Ⓑ 4
- Ⓒ 5
- Ⓓ 6

7. $8,200 - y = 5,600$
- Ⓐ 2,600
- Ⓑ 2,700
- Ⓒ 2,800
- Ⓓ 2,900

8. $99 \div y = 33$
- Ⓐ 66
- Ⓑ 33
- Ⓒ 9
- Ⓓ 3

9. $829 + y = 1,658$
- Ⓐ 2
- Ⓑ 829
- Ⓒ 855
- Ⓓ 1,283

10. $170 + y = 200$
- Ⓐ 3
- Ⓑ 30
- Ⓒ 300
- Ⓓ 3,000

Solving for the Variable

Solve the problems below.

1. Solve for y. $x = 3$.

   $y = 3x + 5$

   (A) 8
   (B) 11
   (C) 14
   (D) 45

2. Solve for y. $x = 8$.

   $y = 2x + 1$

   (A) 17
   (B) 15
   (C) 11
   (D) 3

3. Solve for y. $x = 4$.

   $y = 5x$

   (A) 25
   (B) 20
   (C) 15
   (D) 10

4. Solve for y. $x = 9$.

   $y = 9x + 9$

   (A) 18
   (B) 81
   (C) 90
   (D) 190

5. Solve for y. $x = 6$.

   $y = 4x + 2$

   (A) 6
   (B) 12
   (C) 24
   (D) 26

6. Solve for y. $x = 10$.

   $y = 3x$

   (A) 3
   (B) 10
   (C) 13
   (D) 30

7. Solve for y. $x = 5$.

   $y = 4x - 7$

   (A) 13
   (B) 16
   (C) 27
   (D) 39

8. Solve for y. $x = 3$.

   $y = 6x - 11$

   (A) 6
   (B) 7
   (C) 29
   (D) 39

9. Solve for y. $x = 4$.

   $y = 3x + 12$

   (A) 12
   (B) 19
   (C) 24
   (D) 26

10. Solve for y. $x = 8$.

   $y = 8x \div 2$

   (A) 16
   (B) 18
   (C) 32
   (D) 36

Word Problems

Solve the problems below.

1. Mia had 54 stamps in her collection. Which number sentence shows how many stamps she gave to her six friends?

Ⓐ $54 + x = 117$

Ⓑ $54x = 162$

Ⓒ $54 - x = 6$

Ⓓ $54 \div x = 6$

2. George buys a bag with 12 oranges in it. Which number sentence shows how many bags George will have to buy to get 96 oranges?

Ⓐ $12 + x = 96$

Ⓑ $12 \div x = 96$

Ⓒ $12x = 96$

Ⓓ $12 - x = 96$

3. Shari buys 5 bags of groceries every week. Which operation can you use to tell how many bags of groceries Shari will buy in 8 weeks?

Ⓐ addition

Ⓑ subtraction

Ⓒ multiplication

Ⓓ division

4. Monica read 12 books this summer. Gerry read 8 books. Which number sentence tells how many more books Monica read than Gerry?

Ⓐ $12\,x = 8$

Ⓑ $12 - x = 8$

Ⓒ $12 + x = 8$

Ⓓ $12 \div x = 8$

5. Albert has 210 baseball cards. Which number sentence shows how many cards he will have when his brother gives him 35 more?

Ⓐ $210 + 35 = x$

Ⓑ $35 + x = 210$

Ⓒ $35x = 210$

Ⓓ $x \div 35 = 210$

6. Leah spends $35 on lunch every week. Which operation can you use to tell how much money Leah spends on lunch each day of the week?

Ⓐ multiplication

Ⓑ division

Ⓒ addition

Ⓓ subtraction

Word Problems with Functional Relationships

Use the function table to solve the problems below.

Number of Pencils Per Box

12	24	36	48	60
1	2	3	4	5

1. Hugo's class made a function table to show how many pencils were in the boxes in the classroom. If someone has 3 boxes, how many pencils will there be in all?
Ⓐ 48
Ⓑ 36
Ⓒ 24
Ⓓ 12

2. Each student in the class has to tell what the rule of the function table is. Which student response is correct?
Ⓐ add 12
Ⓑ divide by 12
Ⓒ add 24
Ⓓ divide by 24

3. How many pencils are in 1 box?
Ⓐ 36
Ⓑ 24
Ⓒ 12
Ⓓ 6

4. How many pencils are in 6 boxes?
Ⓐ 72
Ⓑ 66
Ⓒ 60
Ⓓ 18

5. How many pencils are in 9 boxes?
Ⓐ 98
Ⓑ 112
Ⓒ 100
Ⓓ 108

6. How many pencils are in 13 boxes?
Ⓐ 160
Ⓑ 156
Ⓒ 150
Ⓓ 134

7. Hugo has 4 boxes and Shara has 6. How many pencils do they have altogether?
Ⓐ 100
Ⓑ 120
Ⓒ 188
Ⓓ 208

8. Milo has 72 pencils. How many boxes of pencils does he have?
Ⓐ 4
Ⓑ 5
Ⓒ 6
Ⓓ 7

Section 6: Measurement and Geometry

Measurement Units and Conversions

Solve the problems below.

1. How many inches are in 10 feet?
- Ⓐ 100 inches
- Ⓑ 112 inches
- Ⓒ 120 inches
- Ⓓ 124 inches

2. How many meters are in 35 millimeters?
- Ⓐ 3,500
- Ⓑ 350
- Ⓒ .35
- Ⓓ .035

3. Which unit would you use to measure the weight of an elephant?
- Ⓐ ounces
- Ⓑ pounds
- Ⓒ tons
- Ⓓ miles

4. Which unit would you use to measure the weight of a mouse?
- Ⓐ ounces
- Ⓑ pounds
- Ⓒ tons
- Ⓓ miles

5. How many hours are in 9 days?
- Ⓐ 116
- Ⓑ 216
- Ⓒ 218
- Ⓓ 221

6. How many minutes are in 5 hours?
- Ⓐ 24
- Ⓑ 240
- Ⓒ 300
- Ⓓ 360

7. How many milligrams are in 15 grams?
- Ⓐ .015
- Ⓑ .15
- Ⓒ 1,500
- Ⓓ 15,000

8. Which unit would **best** measure the distance from your shoulder to your elbow?
- Ⓐ foot
- Ⓑ mile
- Ⓒ gram
- Ⓓ yard

9. Which tool would you use to measure the height of a door?
- Ⓐ measuring cup
- Ⓑ thermometer
- Ⓒ yardstick
- Ⓓ spring scale

10. How many feet are in 7 yards?
- Ⓐ 21
- Ⓑ 24
- Ⓒ 32
- Ⓓ 36

Word Problems with Measurement

Solve the problems below.

1. Gabby is buying new carpet for her bedroom. The room is 18 feet long by 14 feet wide. How much square footage of carpet will Gabby need?

Ⓐ 32 square feet
Ⓑ 56 square feet
Ⓒ 112 square feet
Ⓓ 252 square feet

2. Greg has 30 liters of juice. He divides the juice equally between 5 friends. How many milliliters will each friend have?

Ⓐ 60
Ⓑ 600
Ⓒ 6,000
Ⓓ 60,000

3. Dominick went to Sunset Lake Summer Camp for 7 weeks and 5 days. How many total days was Dominick at camp?

Ⓐ 67
Ⓑ 54
Ⓒ 49
Ⓓ 19

4. Juno's class paints a 525 square foot wall at the school. Which numbers below show the possible dimensions of the wall they painted?

Ⓐ 13 feet × 45 feet
Ⓑ 14 feet × 30 feet
Ⓒ 15 feet × 35 feet
Ⓓ 20 feet × 50 feet

5. Rico prepares a gallon of lemonade for his friends. If each person drinks one cup of lemonade how many people will it serve?

Ⓐ 16
Ⓑ 17
Ⓒ 18
Ⓓ 19

6. Salah spends two and a half hours watching a movie. How many minutes did he spend watching the movie?

Ⓐ 110
Ⓑ 125
Ⓒ 130
Ⓓ 150

Area and Perimeter

Solve the problems below.

1. Find the area.
  - Ⓐ 20 square inches
  - Ⓑ 16 square inches
  - Ⓒ 12 square inches
  - Ⓓ 8 square inches

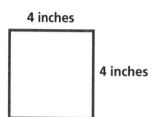
4 inches
4 inches

2. Find the perimeter.
  - Ⓐ 2 inches
  - Ⓑ 5 inches
  - Ⓒ 10 inches
  - Ⓓ 20 inches

2 in.

3. Find the perimeter.
  - Ⓐ 28 cm
  - Ⓑ 22 cm
  - Ⓒ 18 cm
  - Ⓓ 11 cm

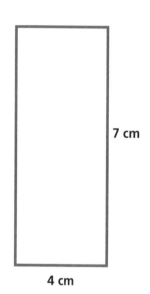
7 cm
4 cm

4. Find the area.
  - Ⓐ 15 square cm
  - Ⓑ 18 square cm
  - Ⓒ 20 square cm
  - Ⓓ 21 square cm

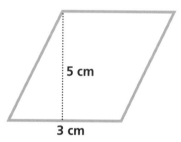
5 cm
3 cm

5. Find the perimeter.
  - Ⓐ 66 cm
  - Ⓑ 50 cm
  - Ⓒ 48 cm
  - Ⓓ 39 cm

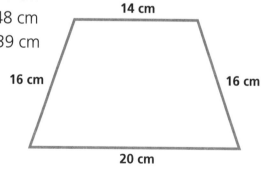
14 cm
16 cm
16 cm
20 cm

6. Find the area.
  - Ⓐ 10 square inches
  - Ⓑ 14 square inches
  - Ⓒ 24 square inches
  - Ⓓ 48 square inches

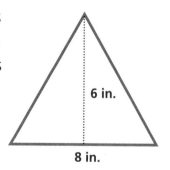
6 in.
8 in.

Radius and Diameter

Solve the problems below. Use the circle to answer questions 1–2.

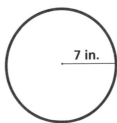

7 in.

1. What is the diameter of the circle?
- Ⓐ 7 inches
- Ⓑ 14 inches
- Ⓒ 21 inches
- Ⓓ 28 inches

2. What is the radius of the circle?
- Ⓐ 7 inches
- Ⓑ 14 inches
- Ⓒ 21 inches
- Ⓓ 28 inches

3. Which formula shows how to find the diameter of a circle?
- Ⓐ $d = \frac{1}{2} r$
- Ⓑ $d = r$
- Ⓒ $d = 2r$
- Ⓓ $d = 4r$

4. What is the radius of a circle with a diameter of 18 cm?
- Ⓐ 6 cm
- Ⓑ 9 cm
- Ⓒ 18 cm
- Ⓓ 36 cm

Use the circle to answer questions 5–6.

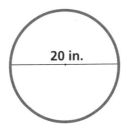

20 in.

5. What is the radius of the circle?
- Ⓐ 40 inches
- Ⓑ 20 inches
- Ⓒ 10 inches
- Ⓓ 5 inches

6. What is the diameter of the circle?
- Ⓐ 40 inches
- Ⓑ 20 inches
- Ⓒ 10 inches
- Ⓓ 5 inches

7. Which formula shows how to find the radius of a circle?
- Ⓐ $r = 3d$
- Ⓑ $r = 2d$
- Ⓒ $r = d$
- Ⓓ $r = \frac{1}{2} d$

8. What is the diameter of a circle that has a 6-inch radius?
- Ⓐ 12 inches
- Ⓑ 10 inches
- Ⓒ 6 inches
- Ⓓ 3 inches

Triangles

Solve the problems below.

1. Which shows a right triangle?

   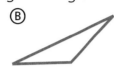

2. What kind of triangle is shown?
- Ⓐ isosceles triangle
- Ⓑ scalene triangle
- Ⓒ right triangle
- Ⓓ equilateral triangle

3. Which triangle has an obtuse angle?

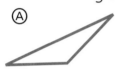   

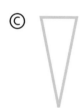   

4. What kind of triangle has three angles of the same measurement?
- Ⓐ scalene triangle
- Ⓑ equilateral triangle
- Ⓒ isosceles triangle
- Ⓓ right triangle

5. Which shows an isosceles angle?

   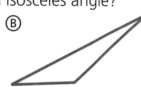

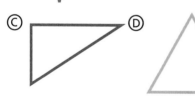

6. What kind of triangle is shown?
- Ⓐ isosceles triangle
- Ⓑ scalene triangle
- Ⓒ right triangle
- Ⓓ equilateral triangle

7. What kind of triangle has two sides the same length?
- Ⓐ isosceles triangle
- Ⓑ scalene triangle
- Ⓒ right triangle
- Ⓓ equilateral triangle

8. What does a right triangle have that other triangles do **not**?
- Ⓐ an acute angle
- Ⓑ an obtuse angle
- Ⓒ a right angle
- Ⓓ all sides the same length

Polygons

Solve the problems below.

1. Which polygon has the greatest number of sides?
  Ⓐ trapezoid
  Ⓑ hexagon
  Ⓒ pentagon
  Ⓓ octagon

2. Which figure does **not** have bilateral symmetry?

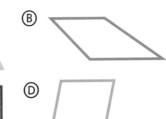

3. Which two figures are congruent?

  Ⓐ

  Ⓑ

  Ⓒ

  Ⓓ

4. Which figure has two more sides than a rhombus?
  Ⓐ trapezoid
  Ⓑ octagon
  Ⓒ pentagon
  Ⓓ hexagon

5. Which figure is congruent to the one shown?

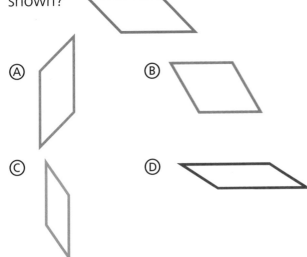

6. Which figure shows symmetry?

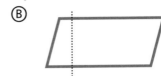

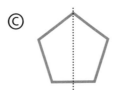

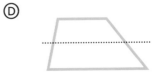

Solid Figures

Solve the problems below.

1. Which solid figure can be made from this net?

ⓐ triangular prism

ⓑ cone

ⓒ cube

ⓓ rectangular prism

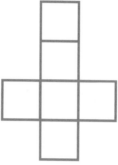

2. Which figure has 6 vertices?

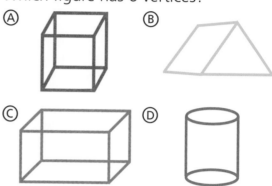

3. Which figure has the same number of sides and edges as the figure shown?

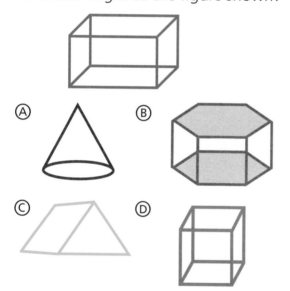

4. Which solid figure can be made from this net?

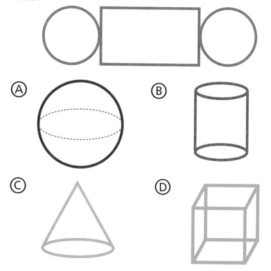

5. Which figure has bilateral symmetry?

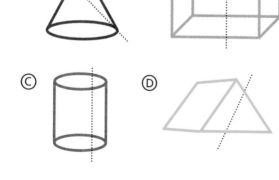

6. Which figure has the same number of faces as the figure shown?

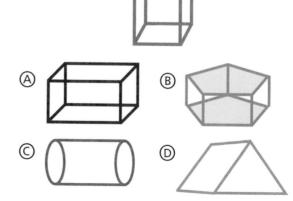

Graphs

Use the graph to solve the problems below.

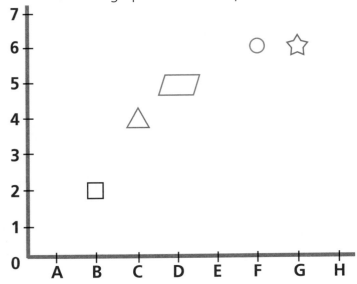

1. What shape is located at C, 4 on the graph?
  Ⓐ square
  Ⓑ triangle
  Ⓒ rhombus
  Ⓓ circle

2. Where is the star located?
  Ⓐ G, 6
  Ⓑ D, 5
  Ⓒ B, 2
  Ⓓ F, 6

3. What can you find at location B, 2?
  Ⓐ square
  Ⓑ triangle
  Ⓒ rhombus
  Ⓓ circle

4. You want to add a heart to the graph. Where can you place it?
  Ⓐ B, 2
  Ⓑ C, 4
  Ⓒ D, 3
  Ⓓ F, 6

5. Where is the circle located?
  Ⓐ B, 2
  Ⓑ C, 4
  Ⓒ D, 5
  Ⓓ F, 6

6. Which location has a shape located on it?
  Ⓐ G, 6
  Ⓑ C, 1
  Ⓒ D, 4
  Ⓓ A, 7

Section 7: Statistics, Data Analysis, and Probability

Likelihood of Events

Use the picture to answer questions 1–3.

1. What is the likelihood that a top will be picked from the box?
Ⓐ certain
Ⓑ likely
Ⓒ improbable
Ⓓ impossible

2. What is the likelihood that a ball will be pulled from the box?
Ⓐ certain
Ⓑ likely
Ⓒ improbable
Ⓓ impossible

3. Which ratio shows the likelihood that a bear will be pulled from the box?
Ⓐ 2:15
Ⓑ 5:30
Ⓒ 8:15
Ⓓ 15:15

Use the picture to answer questions 4–7.

4. What is the likelihood that the spinner will land on a striped section?
Ⓐ certain
Ⓑ likely
Ⓒ improbable
Ⓓ impossible

5. Which ratio shows the probability of the spinner landing on a gray section?
Ⓐ 1:2
Ⓑ 2:2
Ⓒ 2:8
Ⓓ 1:8

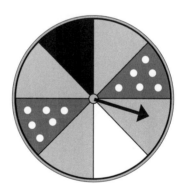

6. Which section is the spinner most likely to land on?
Ⓐ gray
Ⓑ black
Ⓒ white
Ⓓ polka-dotted

7. Which two sections is the spinner equally likely to land on?
Ⓐ gray and white
Ⓑ white and black
Ⓒ black and polka dot
Ⓓ polka dot and gray

Word Problems with Probability

Solve the problems below.

1. Mikey gets three chances to throw a dart at the fair and break a balloon. He misses when he throws the first two darts. Which ratio shows the likelihood that he will hit the balloon on the last turn?

Ⓐ 0:3
Ⓑ 1:3
Ⓒ 2:3
Ⓓ 3:3

2. Sally has a box of crayons. There are 10 crayons in the box. Four of the crayons are red, two are blue, and one is green. What is the likelihood that she will pick a red crayon from the box the next time she picks a crayon?

Ⓐ 1:10
Ⓑ 2:10
Ⓒ 4:10
Ⓓ 10:10

3. Mr. Mee goes to the park. He sees four birds, two dogs, and ten squirrels. What is the likelihood that he will see the same number of animals if he goes to the park tomorrow?

Ⓐ certain
Ⓑ likely
Ⓒ improbable
Ⓓ impossible

4. Jack labels four papers with A, B, C, and D. He puts the papers in a hat. What is the likelihood that he will pull a C from the hat?

Ⓐ 1:4
Ⓑ 2:4
Ⓒ 3:4
Ⓓ 4:4

5. Peggy has three blue socks, six green socks, and eight yellow socks. What is the likelihood that she will pull a yellow sock from her drawer?

Ⓐ 6:17
Ⓑ 8:17
Ⓒ 3:17
Ⓓ 1:17

6. Mae has a pocket full of change. She has 12 pennies, three nickels, eight dimes, and seven quarters. What is the likelihood that she will pull out a quarter from her pocket?

Ⓐ 12:30
Ⓑ 3:30
Ⓒ 8:30
Ⓓ 7:30

Collecting Data

Solve the problems below.

1. You want to know how many students in your class like popcorn. What is the easiest way to find out?
- Ⓐ take a vote
- Ⓑ serve ice cream
- Ⓒ serve popcorn
- Ⓓ make a chart

2. The following graph tells the number of students in a class who like apricots. What would be a good title for the chart?

Fruit	Tally	Number
Apricots	卌 III	8

- Ⓐ Apricots
- Ⓑ Votes
- Ⓒ Students Who Like Apricots
- Ⓓ 8 Vote Yes

3. What kind of graph would be **best** for showing how the population of bears and wolves compares over a three-year period?
- Ⓐ tally chart
- Ⓑ line plot
- Ⓒ bar graph
- Ⓓ double bar graph

4. You toss a coin 10 times. Which shows the **least likely** result of the coin toss?
- Ⓐ 5 heads, 5 tails
- Ⓑ 4 heads, 6 tails
- Ⓒ 7 heads, 3 tails
- Ⓓ 10 heads, 0 tails

5. What kind of chart is **best** for keeping track of the items pulled from this bag?

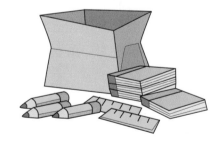

- Ⓐ line plot
- Ⓑ bar graph
- Ⓒ pie chart
- Ⓓ line graph

6. What kind of chart is **best** for displaying the number of people who go to a movie theater each day during one week?
- Ⓐ probability ratio
- Ⓑ bar graph
- Ⓒ pie chart
- Ⓓ tally chart

Tally Charts

Use the tally chart below to answer questions 1–3.

1. Jamal's class counted up the number of pets they have at home. How many pets do Jamal's classmates have?

Ⓐ 19
Ⓑ 9
Ⓒ 10
Ⓓ 5

Pets

Dog	JHT IIII
Cat	JHT
Fish	JHT

2. What kind of pet does Jamal have?

Ⓐ dog
Ⓑ cat
Ⓒ fish
Ⓓ cannot tell

3. How many more dogs do students have than fish?

Ⓐ 9
Ⓑ 5
Ⓒ 4
Ⓓ 2

Use the tally chart below to answer questions 4–6.

4. How many rainy days were there in summer?

Ⓐ 11
Ⓑ 7
Ⓒ 5
Ⓓ 4

Number of Rainy Days

Spring	JHT JHT I
Summer	JHT II
Fall	JHT
Winter	IIII

5. How many rainy days were there in the whole year?

Ⓐ 11
Ⓑ 24
Ⓒ 27
Ⓓ 32

6. How many rainy days were in fall and winter together?

Ⓐ 11
Ⓑ 9
Ⓒ 7
Ⓓ 5

Mean, Mode, Median, and Range

Use the numbers below to answer questions 1–4.
Round up or down as needed.

> 77, 79, 80, 80, 80, 82, 82, 85, 91, 94, 99

1. What is the range of the number set?
- (A) 22
- (B) 77
- (C) 88
- (D) 99

2. What is the mean of the numbers?
- (A) 77
- (B) 82
- (C) 84
- (D) 99

3. What is the median of the numbers?
- (A) 77
- (B) 82
- (C) 84
- (D) 99

4. What is the mode of the numbers?
- (A) 80
- (B) 82
- (C) 84
- (D) 99

Use the numbers below to answer questions 5–8.
Round up or down as needed.

> 8, 9, 9, 10, 10, 11, 12, 12, 12, 13, 13

5. What is the range of the number set?
- (A) 2
- (B) 5
- (C) 8
- (D) 13

6. What is the mean of the numbers?
- (A) 5
- (B) 8
- (C) 11
- (D) 12

7. What is the median of the numbers?
- (A) 8
- (B) 11
- (C) 12
- (D) 13

8. What is the mode of the numbers?
- (A) 8
- (B) 11
- (C) 12
- (D) 13

Bar Graphs

The bar graph shows the number of snakes and lizards in a desert over a period of five years.
Use the bar graph to solve the problems below.

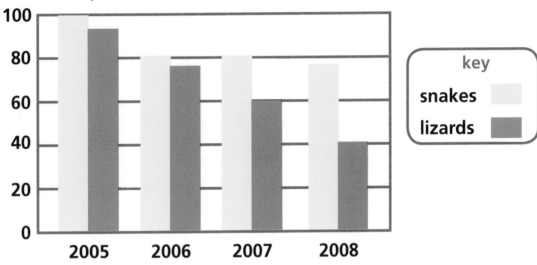

Populations of Snakes and Lizards

key
snakes
lizards

1. How many snakes were there in 2006?
Ⓐ 80
Ⓑ 75
Ⓒ 70
Ⓓ 60

2. What does the graph say about the population of lizards?
Ⓐ It is increasing.
Ⓑ It is decreasing slower than snakes.
Ⓒ It is decreasing faster than snakes.
Ⓓ It stays the same each year.

3. What does the graph say about the population of snakes?
Ⓐ It is increasing.
Ⓑ It is decreasing slower than lizards.
Ⓒ It is decreasing faster than lizards.
Ⓓ It stays the same each year.

4. In what year was the snake population the lowest?
Ⓐ 2005
Ⓑ 2006
Ⓒ 2007
Ⓓ 2008

5. How many lizards were there in 2005?
Ⓐ 100
Ⓑ 95
Ⓒ 80
Ⓓ 75

6. In what year was the difference between the number of snakes and the number of lizards the greatest?
Ⓐ 2008
Ⓑ 2007
Ⓒ 2006
Ⓓ 2005

Line Plots

The line plot shows the math scores of students in Lesley's class.
Use the line plot to solve the problems.

Math Scores

```
                  X     X
                  X     X
      X           X     X
      X     X     X     X     X           X
  X   X     X     X     X     X     X     X     X
  77  79    82    83    85    87    90    92    93
```

1. What was the lowest score that someone got on the test?

Ⓐ 93
Ⓑ 85
Ⓒ 82
Ⓓ 77

2. How many students received a score of 87?

Ⓐ 1
Ⓑ 2
Ⓒ 3
Ⓓ 5

3. How many students received a score of 79?

Ⓐ 1
Ⓑ 2
Ⓒ 3
Ⓓ 5

4. Which of the following test scores did the most students receive?

Ⓐ 79
Ⓑ 82
Ⓒ 83
Ⓓ 92

5. Which score did three students receive?

Ⓐ 77
Ⓑ 79
Ⓒ 92
Ⓓ 93

6. How many students received scores in the 90s?

Ⓐ 6
Ⓑ 4
Ⓒ 2
Ⓓ 1

Section 8: Mathematical Reasoning

Rounding

Solve the problems below.

1. Which number shows 5,034,228 rounded to the nearest thousands place?
Ⓐ 5,030,000
Ⓑ 5,040,000
Ⓒ 5,034,000
Ⓓ 5,000,000

2. Which shows 8,089.0239 rounded to the nearest thousandth?
Ⓐ 8,000
Ⓑ 8,100
Ⓒ 8,089.023
Ⓓ 8,089.024

3. Which number shows 5,509,033 rounded to the nearest million?
Ⓐ 6,000,000
Ⓑ 5,500,000
Ⓒ 5,000,000
Ⓓ 4,000,000

4. Which shows 4,350,200 rounded to the nearest hundred thousand?
Ⓐ 4,000,000
Ⓑ 4,400,000
Ⓒ 4,350,000
Ⓓ 4,300,000

5. Which shows 15.022 rounded to the nearest tenth?
Ⓐ 20.0
Ⓑ 15.0
Ⓒ 15.1
Ⓓ 10.0

6. Which number shows 27.03 rounded to the tens place?
Ⓐ 27.00
Ⓑ 27.03
Ⓒ 30.00
Ⓓ 30.03

7. Which number shows 82.9149 rounded to the nearest thousandths place?
Ⓐ 82.900
Ⓑ 82.910
Ⓒ 82.914
Ⓓ 82.915

8. Which number shows 960 rounded to the nearest tens place?
Ⓐ 1,000
Ⓑ 970
Ⓒ 960
Ⓓ 950

9. Which number shows 7,859,233 rounded to the nearest ten thousands place?
Ⓐ 8,000,000
Ⓑ 7,900,000
Ⓒ 7,860,000
Ⓓ 7,850,000

10. Which number shows 739.739 rounded to the nearest hundredth?
Ⓐ 740.74
Ⓑ 739.74
Ⓒ 739.73
Ⓓ 700.000

Estimating

Solve the problems below.

1. Estimate to the nearest hundred.

$$700 + 750 =$$

Ⓐ 1,400
Ⓑ 1,450
Ⓒ 1,500
Ⓓ 1,550

2. Estimate to the nearest tenth.

$$8.922 + 2.204 =$$

Ⓐ 11.1
Ⓑ 11.2
Ⓒ 11.11
Ⓓ 11.9

3. Estimate to the nearest hundred.

$$822 \div 2 =$$

Ⓐ 400
Ⓑ 410
Ⓒ 411
Ⓓ 415

4. Estimate to the nearest hundred.

$$3511 \div 5 =$$

Ⓐ 750
Ⓑ 700
Ⓒ 650
Ⓓ 600

5. Estimate to the nearest ten.

$$30 \times 16 =$$

Ⓐ 700
Ⓑ 600
Ⓒ 500
Ⓓ 400

6. Estimate to the nearest ten.

$$89 + 99 =$$

Ⓐ 170
Ⓑ 180
Ⓒ 190
Ⓓ 200

7. Estimate to the nearest million.

$$2,400,499 + 3,840,233 =$$

Ⓐ 4,500,000
Ⓑ 5,000,000
Ⓒ 5,500,000
Ⓓ 6,000,000

8. Estimate to the nearest hundred.

$$323 + 56,000 =$$

Ⓐ 56,000
Ⓑ 56,300
Ⓒ 56,500
Ⓓ 57,000

9. Estimate to the nearest hundred thousand.

$$780,244 + 129,332 =$$

Ⓐ 900,000
Ⓑ 850,000
Ⓒ 800,000
Ⓓ 750,000

10. Estimate to the nearest ten.

$$345 + 345 =$$

Ⓐ 750
Ⓑ 700
Ⓒ 650
Ⓓ 600

Estimating Word Problems

Solve the problems below.

1. Jessica bought a bag of about 1,300 peanuts in it for a party. She buys three more bags the next day. Which shows the approximate number of peanuts Jessica bought for the party?

Ⓐ 6,000
Ⓑ 5,000
Ⓒ 4,000
Ⓓ 3,000

2. Marty swam 3,329 laps last year in the pool. About how many laps did he swim each month?

Ⓐ 100
Ⓑ 200
Ⓒ 300
Ⓓ 400

3. There are 459 stairs at the office building. Jamie walked up 293 stairs. About how many does she have left to climb?

Ⓐ 100
Ⓑ 150
Ⓒ 200
Ⓓ 250

4. Abby guesses how many beans are in a jar at the fair. She guesses there are 5,238. If her guess is low and she is off by 839, what is the approximate number of beans in the jar?

Ⓐ 6,000
Ⓑ 7,000
Ⓒ 8,000
Ⓓ 9,000

5. Matilda needs 50,000 pennies to buy a new video game. She has 22,336 pennies saved so far. About how many more does she need?

Ⓐ 25,000
Ⓑ 30,000
Ⓒ 35,000
Ⓓ 40,000

6. Over the summer, Jonah read a 836-page book, a 487-page book, and a 665-page book. About how many pages did he read in all?

Ⓐ 1,700
Ⓑ 1,800
Ⓒ 1,900
Ⓓ 2,000

Estimating or Finding the Exact Answer

Solve the problems below.

1. A big parade needs about 500,000 bags of confetti. They ask hundreds of schools around the country to donate confetti. Do the parade planners need to tell the schools an exact number of bags of confetti to donate, or can they give an estimate?

Ⓐ estimate
Ⓑ find exact answer
Ⓒ neither estimate nor find exact answer
Ⓓ It does not matter.

2. A teacher needs to give a study guide to each child who visits her classroom. She knows that 19 students will visit on Monday and 32 students will visit on Tuesday. Should she use an estimate or an exact number to find out how many study guides she needs?

Ⓐ estimate
Ⓑ find exact answer
Ⓒ neither estimate nor find exact answer
Ⓓ It does not matter.

3. Mr. Gonzalez needs about $50 to buy bushes for the school. He has more than twice that amount. Does he need to know the exact amount or an estimate of how much the bushes will cost?

Ⓐ estimate
Ⓑ find exact answer
Ⓒ neither estimate nor find exact answer
Ⓓ It does not matter.

4. Sonya is mixing a drink that requires you start by putting crushed ice in half of the glass. How should Sonya find the number of ice cubes she needs to make 4 drinks?

Ⓐ estimate
Ⓑ find exact answer
Ⓒ neither estimate nor find exact answer
Ⓓ It does not matter.

5. Darla's mom is making cupcakes for the entire fourth grade class. How will she know how much flour and sugar to buy?

Ⓐ estimate
Ⓑ find exact answer
Ⓒ neither estimate nor find exact answer
Ⓓ It does not matter.

6. Mrs. Yang needs to collect $100 from the class for a school trip. There are 25 students in her class. How will she know how much to collect from each student?

Ⓐ estimate
Ⓑ find exact answer
Ⓒ neither estimate nor find exact answer
Ⓓ It does not matter.

Checking for Reasonableness

Solve the problems below.

1. Peter estimates that he will need $1,000 for three plane tickets that cost $350 each. Did he make a reasonable estimate that includes enough money for the tickets and the sales tax?

Ⓐ No, he will not have enough money.

Ⓑ Yes, he will have just the right amount.

Ⓒ Yes, but he will have very little left over.

Ⓓ Yes, and he will have a lot of money left over.

2. George is buying bottles of juice for a charity event. About 50 children will be going to the event with their mothers and fathers. George estimates that he should have about 150 bottles of juice. Is his estimate reasonable?

Ⓐ No, he will have a lot less juice than needed.

Ⓑ No, he will have much more juice than needed.

Ⓒ Yes, he will have just about the right number of juice.

Ⓓ There is no way to tell how much juice he will need.

3. It takes Zack about 15 minutes to rake enough leaves to fill one bag. He estimates that it will take him 4 hours to fill 20 bags. Is his estimate reasonable?

Ⓐ No, he should need a little more time to fill 20 bags.

Ⓑ No, he should need about 5 more hours to fill the bags.

Ⓒ No, he will be done about an hour ahead of time.

Ⓓ Yes, his estimate is right.

4. Frank's class does about 4 pages of math exercises during class each day. He estimates that it will take them about 5 weeks to finish the 100-page book of exercises. Is his estimate reasonable?

Ⓐ No, the class will take an extra 2 weeks to finish the book.

Ⓑ No, the class will take an extra 2 days to finish the book.

Ⓒ Yes, his estimate is correct.

Ⓓ There is no way to estimate when the class will finish the book.

Too Much, Not Enough Information

Answer the questions below to tell if the word problems give too much information, not enough information, or just the right amount of information to solve the problem.

1. Michael planted 3 rows of corn, 4 rows of cauliflower, 5 rows of carrots, and 8 rows of tomatoes. How many individual carrots and cauliflower did Michael plant?
Ⓐ too much information
Ⓑ not enough information
Ⓒ just the right amount of information
Ⓓ none of the above

2. Sasha read four books in June, three books in July, seven books in August, and four books in September. How many books did Sasha read during the months of June through September?
Ⓐ too much information
Ⓑ not enough information
Ⓒ just the right amount of information
Ⓓ none of the above

Use the chart for questions 3–4.

Week	Number of Cars
Week 1	1,502
Week 2	1,428
Week 3	1,529
Week 4	1,443

3. The chart shows the number of cars that went through the tunnel during four weeks. How many cars went through the tunnel during Week 2?
Ⓐ too much information
Ⓑ not enough information
Ⓒ just the right amount of information
Ⓓ none of the above

4. How many cars went through the tunnel every Friday during the month?
Ⓐ too much information
Ⓑ not enough information
Ⓒ just the right amount of information
Ⓓ none of the above

Choosing the Operation

Choose the operation needed to solve each word problem below.

1. Warren peeled 1,308 potatoes for the soup kitchen. Then he boiled 582 of them. How many peeled potatoes did Warren have left?

Ⓐ addition
Ⓑ subtraction
Ⓒ multiplication
Ⓓ division

2. The soup kitchen served 829 people for lunch and 1,230 people for dinner. How many people did the soup kitchen serve in one day?

Ⓐ addition
Ⓑ subtraction
Ⓒ multiplication
Ⓓ division

3. The chef at the soup kitchen had 3,000 cloves of garlic. He used 45 cloves in each meal. How many meals did the chef make with the garlic?

Ⓐ addition
Ⓑ subtraction
Ⓒ multiplication
Ⓓ division

4. The musical is performed 3 times a day. How many times will the musical be performed in 2 months?

Ⓐ addition
Ⓑ subtraction
Ⓒ multiplication
Ⓓ division

5. The theater has 500 seats. If every show sells out, how many seats are filled over the course of a week?

Ⓐ addition
Ⓑ subtraction
Ⓒ multiplication
Ⓓ division

6. Marah spends $30 to see a show three times. How much does it cost to see the show?

Ⓐ addition
Ⓑ subtraction
Ⓒ multiplication
Ⓓ division

Elapsed Time

Solve the problems below.

1. Class starts at 1:23 and ends at 2:05. How long is class?
Ⓐ 31 minutes
Ⓑ 32 minutes
Ⓒ 33 minutes
Ⓓ 42 minutes

2. Sleepaway camp starts on Monday at 9:00 AM. It ends on Friday at 5:00 PM. How many hours is camp?
Ⓐ 8
Ⓑ 96
Ⓒ 104
Ⓓ 120

3. Sue put the pot on the stove at 5:15. The water started boiling at 5:26. How long did it take for the water to start boiling?
Ⓐ 9 minutes
Ⓑ 10 minutes
Ⓒ 11 minutes
Ⓓ 12 minutes

4. Mr. Marsh dropped off his dog at the kennel at 4:30 on Thursday afternoon. He picked up the dog at 11:00 Saturday morning. How many hours was the dog at the kennel?
Ⓐ $44\frac{1}{2}$
Ⓑ $42\frac{1}{2}$
Ⓒ $30\frac{1}{2}$
Ⓓ $2\frac{1}{2}$

5. The movie previews started at 5:32. They ended at 5:37. How long were the previews?
Ⓐ 5 seconds
Ⓑ 5 minutes
Ⓒ 5 hours
Ⓓ 5 days

6. Sandra mailed a package at 3:30 on Tuesday afternoon. It was delivered at 3:30 on Thursday. How long did the package take to be delivered?
Ⓐ $2\frac{1}{2}$ days
Ⓑ $1\frac{1}{2}$ days
Ⓒ 24 hours
Ⓓ 48 hours

Money

Solve the problems below.

1. Greg has three dollar bills, three quarters, five dimes, seven nickels, and two pennies. How much money does he have?
   - Ⓐ $3.62
   - Ⓑ $4.62
   - Ⓒ $4.77
   - Ⓓ $5.62

2. Jules has four 20-dollar bills, three 5-dollar bills, two quarters, and eight nickels. How much money does he have?
   - Ⓐ $95.90
   - Ⓑ $94.90
   - Ⓒ $94.20
   - Ⓓ $93.40

3. Mrs. Chen has four 10-dollar bills, four one-dollar bills, four quarters, and four dimes. How much money does she have?
   - Ⓐ $44.40
   - Ⓑ $44.44
   - Ⓒ $45.40
   - Ⓓ $45.60

4. Melissa has 14 quarters, 15 dimes, 12 nickels, and five pennies. How much money does she have?
   - Ⓐ $4.55
   - Ⓑ $4.65
   - Ⓒ $5.55
   - Ⓓ $5.65

5. Pedro has six quarters, eight dimes, 19 nickels, and 35 pennies. How much money does he have?
   - Ⓐ $2.60
   - Ⓑ $3.60
   - Ⓒ $3.80
   - Ⓓ $4.60

6. Paige has three 20-dollar bills and 136 pennies. How much money does she have?
   - Ⓐ $60.36
   - Ⓑ $61.30
   - Ⓒ $61.35
   - Ⓓ $61.36

7. Corin has 15 quarters, 32 nickels, and 218 pennies. How much money does she have?
   - Ⓐ $7.53
   - Ⓑ $8.53
   - Ⓒ $8.63
   - Ⓓ $9.53

8. Mrs. Yee has six 10-dollar bills, twelve 5-dollar bills, 18 quarters, and 21 dimes. How much money does she have?
   - Ⓐ $100.60
   - Ⓑ $111.26
   - Ⓒ $126.60
   - Ⓓ $136.60

Section 9: Test

Solve the problems below.

1. 5,300,204 + 2,300,202 =
  Ⓐ 7,700,402
  Ⓑ 7,600,406
  Ⓒ 7,600,102
  Ⓓ 7,422,011

2. 5,931 ÷ 3 =
  Ⓐ 1,977
  Ⓑ 1,877
  Ⓒ 1,711
  Ⓓ 1,611

3. 892 × 91 =
  Ⓐ 81,722
  Ⓑ 81,272
  Ⓒ 81,172
  Ⓓ 81,072

4. 9,000,210 − 2,899,231 =
  Ⓐ 6,110,979
  Ⓑ 6,110,797
  Ⓒ 6,109,031
  Ⓓ 6,100,979

5. What is the rule of the function table?

2	4	6	8	10
1	2	3	4	5

  Ⓐ add 2
  Ⓑ divide by 2
  Ⓒ multiply by 2
  Ⓓ subtract 2

6. What is the area of the figure?

5 inches

3 inches

  Ⓐ 8 square inches
  Ⓑ 8 square cm
  Ⓒ 15 square inches
  Ⓓ 15 square cm

7. Round the number below to the nearest hundred thousand.

   9,352,034

  Ⓐ 9,300,000
  Ⓑ 9,350,000
  Ⓒ 9,400,000
  Ⓓ 9,450,000

8. How many inches are in 12 feet?
  Ⓐ 144 inches
  Ⓑ 124 inches
  Ⓒ 96 inches
  Ⓓ 72 inches

9. What solid can be made by folding this figure?

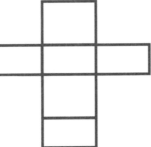

- Ⓐ triangular prism
- Ⓑ rectangular prism
- Ⓒ cube
- Ⓓ hexagonal prism

10. There are 12 crayons in a box. Of these, 11 are white. What is the probability that you will pick a color other than white?

- Ⓐ certain
- Ⓑ likely
- Ⓒ improbable
- Ⓓ impossible

11. There are 5 marbles in a bag. The marbles are red, blue, green, yellow, and orange. What is the probability that you will pick an orange marble from the bag?

- Ⓐ 1:5
- Ⓑ 2:5
- Ⓒ 5:5
- Ⓓ 5:1

12. School starts at 8:45 and goes until 2:55. How many minutes long is the school day?

- Ⓐ 380
- Ⓑ 375
- Ⓒ 370
- Ⓓ 360

13. Mr. Lee buys books that cost $3.99 and $4.45. How much change does he get back from $20?

- Ⓐ $11.56
- Ⓑ $9.24
- Ⓒ $8.44
- Ⓓ $8.24

14. Sue walks 4 miles on Monday, 3 and a half miles on Tuesday, and 5 miles on Wednesday. How many miles did Sue walk on Thursday and Friday? Do you have too much information, not enough information, or just the right amount of information to answer the question?

- Ⓐ too much information
- Ⓑ not enough information
- Ⓒ just the right amount of information
- Ⓓ none of the above

15. Craig has 15 apples. He gives three to each of his three friends. Which operation would you choose to solve how many each received?

- Ⓐ addition
- Ⓑ subtraction
- Ⓒ multiplication
- Ⓓ division

16. Which property is shown by the number sentence?

$$6(2 + 4) = (6 \times 2) + (6 \times 4)$$

- Ⓐ identity
- Ⓑ associative
- Ⓒ commutative
- Ⓓ distributive

17. Which number is missing from the pattern below?

8,305, 8,310, 8,315, _____, 8,325

Ⓐ 8,320
Ⓑ 8,315
Ⓒ 8,310
Ⓓ 8,305

18. $\frac{2}{5} + \frac{3}{5} =$

Ⓐ $\frac{2}{5}$
Ⓑ $\frac{3}{5}$
Ⓒ $\frac{4}{5}$
Ⓓ 1

19. Which fraction is shown?

Ⓐ $\frac{4}{7}$
Ⓑ $\frac{5}{7}$
Ⓒ $\frac{6}{7}$
Ⓓ $\frac{7}{7}$

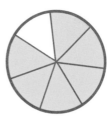

20. Jack buys five tickets for $10.75 each. How much change does he get from $100?

Ⓐ $46.25
Ⓑ $49.20
Ⓒ $53.75
Ⓓ $54.25

21. Round the number below to the nearest hundredth.

829.245

Ⓐ 800
Ⓑ 800.245
Ⓒ 829.24
Ⓓ 829.25

22. 78.20 × 8.23 =

Ⓐ 543.586
Ⓑ 563.685
Ⓒ 643.586
Ⓓ 643.856

23. What is the radius of the circle?

Ⓐ 2 cm
Ⓑ 4 cm
Ⓒ 6 cm
Ⓓ 8 cm

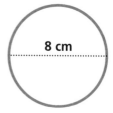

8 cm

24. What is the diameter of the circle?

Ⓐ 1.5 inches
Ⓑ 3 inches
Ⓒ 6 inches
Ⓓ 12 inches

3 in.

25. What is the perimeter of the figure?

Ⓐ 12 cm
Ⓑ 15 cm
Ⓒ 60 cm
Ⓓ 180 cm

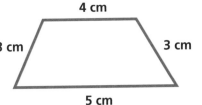

26. What is the mean of the numbers below?

34, 37, 38, 42, 45, 56

Ⓐ 22
Ⓑ 38
Ⓒ 40
Ⓓ 42

27. What is the median of the numbers below?

14, 14, 19, 20, 21, 22, 22

Ⓐ 22
Ⓑ 20
Ⓒ 18
Ⓓ 14

28. What is the mode of the number set below?

8, 8, 10, 10, 11, 12, 12, 12

Ⓐ 8
Ⓑ 10
Ⓒ 11
Ⓓ 12

29. What is the **best** tool for measuring the length of a toothbrush?

Ⓐ ruler
Ⓑ measuring cup
Ⓒ meter stick
Ⓓ thermometer

30. Jill's new patio is 15 feet by 18 feet. What is the area of her new patio?

Ⓐ 270 square feet
Ⓑ 270 feet
Ⓒ 33 square feet
Ⓓ 66 square feet

31. Which kind of figure is shown?

Ⓐ cylinder
Ⓑ cube
Ⓒ cone
Ⓓ sphere

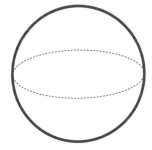

32. Mr. Kane went to the store at 4:00. He returned home at 6:30. How long was Mr. Kane gone?

Ⓐ 2 hours
Ⓑ 2 $\frac{1}{2}$ hours
Ⓒ 3 hours
Ⓓ 3 $\frac{1}{2}$ hours

Answer Key

Page 8
1. B
2. D
3. B
4. A

Page 9
1. C
2. D
3. D
4. B

Page 10
1. B
2. C
3. C
4. B

Page 11
1. B
2. D
3. A
4. B

Page 12
1. B
2. A
3. C
4. B
5. A

Page 13
1. A
2. B
3. C
4. B

Page 14
1. A
2. C
3. D
4. C

Page 15
1. A
2. A
3. C
4. B
5. C
6. D

Page 16
1. B
2. A
3. C
4. B

Page 17
1. D
2. C
3. B
4. B

Page 18
1. A
2. B
3. C
4. B

Page 19
1. B
2. D
3. A
4. C
5. B
6. B

Page 20
1. C
2. A
3. B
4. B

Page 21
1. C
2. A
3. B
4. C

Page 22
1. B
2. C
3. C
4. B
5. B

Page 23
1. C
2. C
3. D
4. B
5. C

Page 24
1. C
2. B
3. D
4. A
5. C

Page 25
1. D
2. C
3. C
4. D

Page 26
1. B
2. C
3. B
4. A

Page 27
1. B
2. D
3. A
4. C
5. C
6. A

7. B
8. D

Page 28
1. C
2. A
3. D
4. B
5. A
6. C
7. B
8. C
9. A
10. D

Page 29
1. B
2. C
3. A
4. D
5. C
6. A
7. A
8. D
9. A
10. D

Page 30
1. A
2. C
3. D
4. C
5. D
6. A
7. B
8. B
9. C
10. D

Page 31
1. B
2. D
3. A
4. B
5. C
6. A
7. C
8. B
9. D
10. B

Page 32
1. D
2. C
3. C
4. A
5. D
6. B
7. A
8. A

Page 33
1. B
2. A
3. D
4. A
5. C
6. D
7. C
8. B
9. B
10. A

Page 34
1. C
2. A
3. D
4. A
5. B
6. C
7. B
8. A
9. D
10. C
11. C
12. A

Page 35
1. B
2. D
3. A
4. B
5. D
6. C
7. A
8. C
9. B
10. D

Page 36
1. B
2. C
3. D
4. C
5. A
6. C
7. A
8. B
9. C
10. D

Page 37
1. C
2. D
3. A
4. B
5. C
6. D
7. A
8. C
9. D
10. C
11. B
12. D

Page 38
1. A
2. C
3. B
4. A
5. C
6. A
7. C
8. C
9. D
10. A
11. B
12. A

Page 39
1. C
2. A
3. D
4. B
5. A
6. B
7. B
8. C
9. D
10. B
11. A
12. D

Page 40
1. A
2. B
3. B
4. C
5. A
6. C
7. D
8. A
9. C
10. A

Page 41
1. C
2. A
3. A
4. D
5. B
6. C
7. C
8. C
9. D
10. C

Page 42
1. A
2. D
3. C
4. D
5. C
6. B
7. A
8. D
9. C
10. D

Page 43
1. B
2. A
3. C
4. A
5. B
6. C
7. D

8. A
9. B
10. A

Page 44
1. B
2. A
3. C
4. D
5. A
6. C
7. A
8. B
9. C
10. C
11. D
12. B

Page 45
1. D
2. C
3. C
4. A
5. D
6. B
7. B
8. B

Pages 46–49
1. B
2. D
3. B
4. D
5. D
6. C
7. A
8. C
9. B
10. B
11. D
12. A
13. B
14. D
15. B
16. C
17. B
18. B
19. A
20. A
21. C
22. D
23. B
24. C
25. A
26. A
27. B
28. D
29. B
30. A

Page 50
1. B
2. A
3. C
4. D
5. C
6. B
7. A
8. A

Page 51
1. C
2. D
3. B
4. A
5. B
6. D
7. A
8. C
9. D
10. C

Page 52
1. A
2. C
3. B
4. D
5. C
6. A
7. B
8. B
9. C
10. A
11. D
12. B

Page 53
1. B
2. A
3. C
4. B
5. D
6. B
7. A
8. C
9. D
10. C
11. A
12. B

Page 54
1. B
2. D
3. C
4. D
5. C
6. B

Page 55
1. A
2. C
3. B
4. D
5. C
6. A

Page 56
1. C
2. A
3. D
4. B
5. A
6. A
7. C
8. D
9. B
10. C

Page 57
1. D
2. D
3. B

4. B
5. C
6. A
7. B
8. C
9. A
10. D

Page 58
1. B
2. D
3. C
4. D
5. C
6. B
7. C
8. B

Page 59
1. B
2. C
3. A
4. D
5. A
6. B
7. C
8. B
9. C
10. A

Page 60
1. A
2. A
3. D
4. C
5. C
6. B
7. B
8. B
9. D
10. C

Page 61
1. B
2. B
3. C
4. C
5. A
6. B
7. B
8. D

Page 62
1. C
2. B
3. A
4. C
5. D
6. C
7. A
8. D
9. B
10. B

Page 63
1. C
2. A
3. B
4. C
5. D
6. D
7. A

8. B
9. C
10. C

Page 64
1. D
2. C
3. C
4. B
5. A
6. B

Page 65
1. B
2. B
3. C
4. A
5. D
6. B
7. B
8. C

Page 66
1. C
2. D
3. C
4. A
5. B
6. C
7. D
8. A
9. C
10. A

Page 67
1. D
2. C
3. B
4. C
5. A
6. D

Page 68
1. B
2. D
3. B
4. A
5. A
6. C

Page 69
1. B
2. A
3. C
4. B
5. C
6. B
7. D
8. A

Page 70
1. C
2. D
3. A
4. B
5. A
6. B
7. A
8. C

Page 71
1. D
2. B
3. C
4. D
5. A
6. C

Page 72
1. C
2. B
3. D
4. B
5. B
6. A

Page 73
1. B
2. A
3. A
4. C
5. D
6. A

Page 74
1. C
2. B
3. B
4. D
5. A
6. A
7. B

Page 75
1. B
2. C
3. C
4. A
5. B
6. D

Page 76
1. A
2. C
3. D
4. D
5. A
6. B

Page 77
1. A
2. D
3. C
4. B
5. C
6. B

Page 78
1. A
2. C
3. B
4. A
5. B
6. C
7. B
8. C

Page 79
1. A
2. C
3. B
4. D
5. B
6. A

Page 80
1. D
2. B
3. C
4. C
5. B
6. B

Page 81
1. C
2. D
3. A
4. B
5. B
6. C
7. D
8. C
9. C
10. B

Page 82
1. C
2. A
3. A
4. B
5. B
6. C
7. D
8. B
9. A
10. B

Page 83
1. B
2. C
3. B
4. A
5. B
6. D

Page 84
1. A
2. B
3. D
4. A
5. A
6. B

Page 85
1. A
2. C
3. A
4. C

Page 86
1. B
2. C
3. A
4. B

Page 87
1. B
2. A
3. D
4. C
5. C
6. D

Page 88
1. D
2. C
3. C
4. B
5. B
6. D

Page 89
1. B
2. A
3. C
4. D
5. B
6. D
7. A
8. C

Pages 90–93
1. B
2. A
3. C
4. D
5. B
6. C
7. C
8. A
9. B
10. C
11. A
12. C
13. A
14. B
15. D
16. D
17. A
18. D
19. C
20. A
21. D
22. C
23. B
24. C
25. B
26. D
27. B
28. D
29. A
30. A
31. D
32. B